Winning Resources and Support

The Open University

Business School

Book 2

Communicating Your Case for Support

Prepared for the course team by Jane Isaacs and
Terry O'Sullivan

COURSE TEAM

Dr Marylyn Carrigan, *Course Chair*

Barry Jones, *Course Manager*

Sue Treacy, *Course Team Assistant*

Carrick Allison, *Institute of Fundraising*

Sam Cooper, *OU Business School Programme Coordinator*

Joan Hunt, *OU Business School Regional Manager*

Amanda Shepard, *Institute of Fundraising*

Dr Terry O'Sullivan, *Senior Lecturer in Management*

Production Team

Simon Ashby, *Editor*

Paul Beeby, *Media Project Manager*

Martin Brazier, *Graphic Designer*

Holly Clements, *Picture research and Rights clearance*

Roy Lawrence, *Graphic Artist*

Gill MacIver, *Media Assistant*

David Richings, *Materials procurement*

Kristoff van Leeuwen, *Media Assistant*

Critical Readers

Sam Cooper, *Programme Coordinator*

Gail Delvin-Jones, *Eranda Foundation*

Chris Durkin, *University of Northampton*

Acknowledgements

We are grateful to the Institute of Fundraising for its assistance in the development of this course. The course team would like to acknowledge the contribution of the following authors whose work, ideas and creativity in previous courses have helped shape the thinking behind B625 Winning Resources and Support:

Julian Batsleer

Chris Cornforth

Jane Isaacs

Sarabajaya Kumar

Jill Mordaunt

Rob Paton

Alan Thomas

Sue Ward

The Open University
Walton Hall, Milton Keynes
MK7 6AA

First published 2007, Reprinted 2008. This edition 2010.

Copyright © 2007, 2008, 2010 The Open University

Edited and designed by The Open University.

Typeset in India by Alden Prepress Services, Chennai.

Printed in the United Kingdom by Hobbs the Printers Limited, Brunel Road, Totton, Hampshire SO40 3WX.

The paper used in this publication is procured from forests independently certified to the level of Forest Stewardship Council (FSC) principles and criteria. Chain of custody certification allows the tracing of this paper back to specific forest-management units (see www.fsc.org).

ISBN 978 1 8487 3579 8

2.1

CONTENTS

Introduction to Book 2   5

Session 1   Establishing your fundraising case   7

Session 2   Introducing communication   27

Session 3   Preparing your message   59

Session 4   Getting your message across   79

References   116

Acknowledgements   119

INTRODUCTION TO BOOK 2

Communication is one of the most fundamental skills in fundraising. This book considers the subject through the three essential stages of developing a compelling message (establishing a fundraising case), expressing it as effectively as possible (communicating and delivering your message) and sustaining it over time.

The first session builds on the management control loop model introduced in Book 1. The model we develop here, though, is called the 'fundraising cycle' – a management control loop which has been specifically adapted to reflect the process of winning resources and support. The first stage of the cycle involves establishing the fundraising requirements of an organisation by outlining the need to be met, the nature of the service planned to meet it, the rationale for support and the kinds and amount of resources necessary. Combined, these elements constitute the basis for your fundraising case statement. This is the theme of Session 1. A case statement acts as a source for your communications, about either the organisation or the good cause in general, or in support of particular initiatives, events and appeals. The case statement is also valuable as an internal marketing tool, helping to unite the organisation in its view of the direction and purpose of its work and keeping colleagues and board members or trustees 'on message'.

Once a message has been established, the next step is to communicate it effectively. The model of the communication process in Session 2 emphasises the need to find common ground with those with whom we communicate. In practical terms this means considering the different interest groups which together constitute your organisation's audience (the stakeholders discussed in Book 1) and deciding how best to prioritise your communication efforts towards them. Clearly, establishing common ground with your audiences will involve finding out more about them. In many situations this is an informal process, but there are also structured techniques used by market researchers which are useful in finding out about audiences in a more systematic way. The session concludes by introducing some of the most important ones in a way that will help you understand the kinds of information available, and the ways in which it is gathered. Research into fundraising opportunities is likely to be part of your regular work, involving the use of existing sources of information (what we call *secondary* research). For *primary* research, the gathering of new data for specific decisions, you are more likely to want to commission the services of specialist agencies rather than undertaking it yourself. The session aims to equip you with enough understanding to make well-informed decisions in talking to professional researchers and interpreting their findings.

Session 3 concentrates on formulating and delivering messages, using the simple AIDA model – popular with advertising and marketing practitioners since the early twentieth century. The four stages of Attention, Interest, Desire and Action comprise a flexible template which can be adapted to serve a number of communications purposes. Even though the model was developed in the service of selling goods and services for commercial gain, it provides a guide to planning and evaluating persuasive messages aimed at winning a variety of resources and support. In the voluntary sector style, image and language are important to the way in which organisations position themselves in the minds of their supporters. The session outlines some useful guidelines for getting the maximum value from them in communications.

Session 4 surveys a number of different techniques which are available for getting your message across – from using the mass media to reach a potential audience of millions, to face-to-face contact between individuals. Apart from the different costs involved, each of these techniques has its own capabilities and limitations. Deciding an appropriate mix of communications techniques requires a careful balancing of the available resources with the objectives which your organisation needs to achieve.

Session 4 ends with a focus on sustainable communications and campaigning in order to organise the best use of your available resources for communication. It also sets communication in a broader context, including raising public awareness and education; influencing and changing public attitudes; and activities which are intended to influence Government policy or legislation. Charities need to be careful about the role of campaigning in their activities because organisations that are established to pursue political purposes cannot benefit from charitable status. But campaigning and political activity may be carried out by recognised charities as a means of furthering their charitable purposes perfectly legitimately (Charity Commission, 2004). How closely the fundraising function is tied into wider campaigning will vary from one organisation to another. But the two areas often overlap, particularly in smaller organisations, and all fundraisers can benefit from a closer understanding of campaigning not only because of the importance of delivering consistent messages, but also because of the fundraising opportunities it can present.

Session 1
Establishing Your Fundraising Case

CONTENTS

1.1 Introduction   11

1.2 The case for support   11

   1.2.1 The internal function of your case for support   19

   1.2.2 The external function of your case for support   20

1.3 Barriers to stating your case effectively   21

1.4 Summary   25

1 ESTABLISHING YOUR FUNDRAISING CASE

1.1 INTRODUCTION

Developing a case for support is at the heart of the fundraiser's role. If you are unclear about your organisation's identity, whom it serves and what it wants to achieve with the funds you spend your time raising, then you are not likely to be able to convince anyone else that your cause is one they should support.

In this session we will look at how you might go about producing a case for support and what needs to be covered in your initial thinking and discussions with colleagues. Some organisations use the term 'case statement' to describe the document which they produce. Whether or not you use that same terminology, the work involved in developing your case should follow similar principles of good practice. We will look at some examples of fundraising cases and at some of the considerations to bear in mind in establishing or revising your own.

Aims and learning outcomes

The three main aims of this session are:

- to introduce a systematic approach to producing a case for support for a particular event or campaign
- to develop understanding of how to present a proposal which clearly outlines facts and benefits
- to help you to understand how organisations can use fundraising 'case statements' to develop their funding proposals.

After studying this session you should be able to:

- produce a case for support for an organisation or appeal
- clearly outline the facts and benefits of your case
- explain the use of fundraising case statements
- critique a case statement constructively.

1.2 THE CASE FOR SUPPORT

Let's start with a definition: 'A case for support sets out why donors should give to a charity and how donors can contribute to the charity's activities' (Institute of Fundraising, 2006, p. 14). Answering these two questions of 'why' and 'how' is fundamental to planning and implementing effective fundraising. In fact, establishing a case for support is the first stage in the planning model known as the fundraising cycle (Mullin, 2002; Institute of Fundraising, 2006). In order to set the context for our discussion of how to make a case for support, let's start by having a closer look at this model as it relates to the planning control loop.

As we have seen, the general model of planning known as the control loop moves through stages of setting goals and targets, devising and undertaking activities, monitoring results, and making any necessary adjustments as you set goals and targets for the next round. Figure 1.1 shows how this general planning model relates to the fundraising cycle, which features four broad stages of 'Establish the case for support', 'Research', 'Develop the Plan' and 'Monitor and evaluate' (Institute of Fundraising, 2006, p. 12). You may come across different variants of the fundraising cycle as used by other writers (e.g. Elischer, 1998; Kramer, 1998; Rosso, 2003), but what all of them have in common is that the process starts by defining the need you are setting out to meet, how your service meets it, why it's important, and how donors can help. In short, this is the case for support (or case statement), which is the focus for this session.

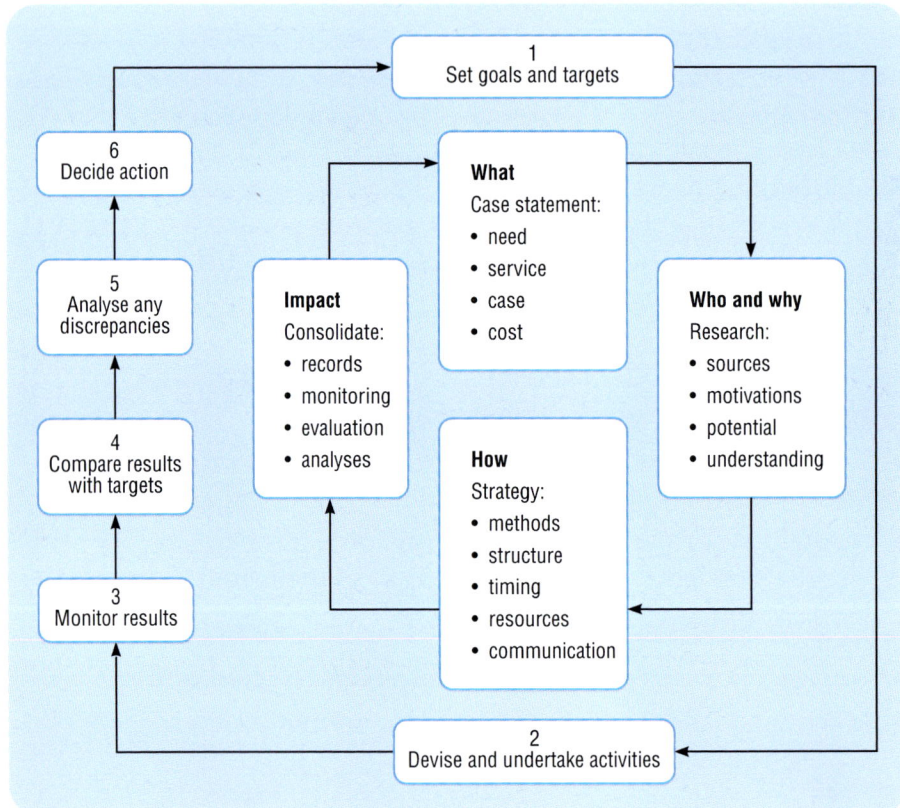

Figure 1.1 Overlaying the 'planning control loop' on the fundraising cyle

Overlaying the planning control loop on the fundraising cycle in Figure 1.1 reveals that the stages in the two models correspond pretty closely. 'Establish the case for support' will include setting 'goals and targets', for example. 'Research' and 'Develop the plan' are roughly the same as 'devise and undertake activities'. The reason why the fundraising cycle model provides two stages here rather than one is that successful fundraising relies so heavily on identifying a target audience of potential donors or funders and understanding their motivations. So, in fundraising planning, the stage of devising and undertaking activities tends to be led by the stage of research into what kind of donors and other sources are likely to be most responsive to the appeal developed in your case for support, and what kind of approaches to them are likely to have most success.

'Monitor and evaluate' in the fundraising cycle aims to control the plan and keep it on course. Monitoring is the process of regularly checking on the progress of a plan as it is being carried out (for example, keeping a record of ticket sales for a fundraising event as the date draws near). It's worth realising that monitoring is just one form of evaluation. Two other forms are assessment and review. Assessment involves evaluating alternative courses of action in advance. For example, if ticket sales are lagging, you might have to assess the alternative options of scaling down the event or encouraging committee members to work harder to sell more tickets in the time available.

'Review' looks back at an activity afterwards, in order to learn lessons for next time. You might decide, looking back at a particular event, like a fundraising dinner, for example, that it needs to be changed in some way to be more effective next time, or even dropped altogether in favour of a fresh idea.

As you can see, the planning control loop breaks 'monitoring and evaluation' down into several more stages – monitoring results, comparing with targets, analysing discrepancies and taking corrective action. This emphasises the importance of monitoring and evaluation in winning resources and support. Unless we build time into projects to analyse and explain why things went well, or not so well, we limit our ability to learn from experience.

Both models present fundraising planning as a cyclical process. This underlines the way in which experience of running one appeal or event builds an organisation's capacity, including its ability to set the right kind of goals and targets for future events and appeals. Mullin (2002, p. 64) puts this well: 'As the funding processes progress and succeed each other, the organisation grows in understanding of itself and its supporters.' This understanding feeds into its ability to articulate the why and how of support in a case statement.

We have seen how planning takes place at different levels, and how strategic, business and operational plans fit into one another. The same can be said of case statements. The most general kind of case statement is at an overall organisational level – relating the why and how of supporting an organisation to its overall mission. At this level, a case statement is independent of any particular event or fundraising technique, but can be adapted into more specific statements to support a wide range of initiatives (in the same way that a strategic plan can lead to a series of more specific business and operational plans). It contains the essential information and arguments which you and your organisation need to share with supporters and funders in order to convince them that you are worth their investment.

ACTIVITY 1.1

Think about your organisation, or one that you are familiar with, and the unique contribution it makes. Now answer the following questions about your chosen organisation and the purpose to which its hard-won resources are put.

Why does the organisation exist?

_____

_____

_____

What is distinctive/different about it?

History of success as Action for democratic
unique knowledge on certain areas
like Swazeland

What does it want to accomplish?

democracy + development in
southern Africa

How does it plan to go about this?

Encourage governments + institutions in
the UK + elsewhere to support it where
democracy is lacking. highlight this + get
those with power to act

What makes the organisation competent to do it?

Links with democratic parties orgs in
target countries, links with NGOs outside
southern Africa. expertise

How is it accountable for what it does?

NEC with officers, members + AGM,
auditors.

_____

Harold J. Seymour, a classic writer on fundraising, described the fundraising case in this way:

> _The case is an expression of the cause, or a clear compelling statement of all the reasons why anyone should consider making a contribution in support of or to advance the cause._

> (Seymour, 1966)

Have you captured that ambition in your statements above?
If so, you now have the beginnings of your fundraising case.
If you can present answers to these fundamental questions
then you can begin to communicate your case to other people.

BOX 1.1

MAKING THE CASE

Iain McMullan, a UK-based fundraiser, explains the importance of making your case:

'This is an absolutely fundamental step – the foundation for everything that follows. Preparing a written document like this allows you to rehearse, polish and develop your case.

If you haven't got clarity yourself – and the buy-in from other parts of the organisation – you will come unstuck further down the line as potential donors and supporters start to probe and question.

It's not about money. People aren't motivated to give by the desire to give money away. The fundamental proposition is what difference your ambitions are going to make, and to whom.'

Box 1.2 gives an example of how one particular organisation – the World YWCA – describes the importance of the case for support to its member organisations around the globe. In fact, its list of what to include in a case statement goes even further than the basic template we have outlined in Activity 1.1 by finishing with a definition of the target audience. Notice how it emphasises the need for a positive story that appeals both to mind and to heart. It also makes the important point that a case statement is primarily an internal document, but provides the inspiration for all the organisation's external communications.

BOX 1.2

YWCA FUNDRAISING – THE CASE FOR SUPPORT

A key ingredient in any successful campaign is the organisation's case for support. This foundation document spells out who you are, who you serve, and what you hope to achieve with the funds to be raised.

The picture it paints is both rational and emotional. The emotional elements speak to the heart; they can tell the story of a person whose life was changed. The rational side illustrates how the gift becomes an investment in the future; statistics are often used. For example, a case for a new literacy programme might be based on statistics illustrating the link between illiteracy and joblessness, and bolstered with an anecdote about a local resident whose quality of life improved dramatically when she learned to read.

Early in the document, the case for support puts forth the organisation's mission statement and vision, which should be very clear. It then uses different literary devices to put forth a persuasive argument for the organisation's goals and objectives.

The case for support is primarily an internal document but proposals, brochures, speeches, videos and other materials are derived from it. The presentation of the case can then be tailored to the interests of the particular audience – an emotive appeal for an individual donor or practical reasoning for a corporate or foundation funder. The case statement usually starts out as a simple document written by members of the staff, a consultant, or a team of volunteers. This initial document is circulated among key members of the campaign team to ensure their complete understanding of and support for the goals of the campaign.

In building a strong and persuasive case for support, focus on your organisation's strengths – those attributes that will make you an attractive philanthropic investment. In addition to building confidence in the organisation, a strong case for support also describes the community's needs. How will a successful campaign enable the YWCA to improve the lives of individuals in its community, strengthen the local economy, and build the neighborhood?

Some may begin the process of developing a case for support by identifying their needs or assets that they currently lack (funding, facilities, people etc.). However, successful campaigns are not based on the organisation's needs for two reasons:

- Your needs will not inspire others to give.
- The most generous charitable gifts are motivated by the donor's genuine belief in your organisation's mission and vision.

When you focus on needs, you adopt a mindset of scarcity.

Philanthropy occurs in a context of abundance.

Characteristics of an effective case for support

- Explains why the fundraising opportunity is an investment that is consistent with the donor's values and interests.
- Does not limit itself to the institution. The most effective cases for support examine issues in society as thoroughly as they describe the institution's programmes. The environment is described through social, geographic, economic, and political factors that affect you and your prospective donors.
- Is accurate. Any claims are fully supported.
- Both rational and emotional. Often human anecdotes appeal to the heart while statistical data reassure the head.
- Is memorable – which is to say that it is brief, to the point, well-organised and meaningful.

- Reads with a sense of urgency, so the donor is convinced to make a gift quickly.

- Evokes positive feelings. Is based on the strengths of the institution, not its 'needs'.

- Concludes with a fundraising goal, and the potential donor's role in helping to achieve it.

Defining the target audience for the case for support

Who is our prospective donor?

Will we appeal to a broad audience, or a closely knit institutional family?

What is the donor's connection to the institution?

What are the concerns and aspirations of the donor?

(Source: World YWCA Common Concern, 2000)

ACTIVITY 1.2

Now look back to the case for support which you began to develop in Activity 1.1. How far does it meet the characteristics of an effective case for support as outlined above? Make brief notes against each of the headings below.

Explains why the fundraising opportunity is an investment that is consistent with the donor's values and interests:

_____

_____

_____

Does not limit itself to the institution/describes the environment:

_____

_____

_____

Is accurate. Any claims are fully supported:

_____

_____

_____

Both rational and emotional. Often human anecdotes appeal to the heart while statistical data reassure the head:

_____

_____

_____

Is memorable which is to say that it is brief, to the point, well organised and meaningful:

_____

_____

_____

Reads with a sense of urgency, so the donor is convinced to make a gift quickly:

_____

_____

_____

Evokes positive feelings. Is based on the strengths of the institution, not its 'needs':

_____

_____

_____

Concludes with a fundraising goal, and the potential donor's role in helping to achieve it:

_____

_____

_____

Your precise response to this activity will depend on the nature of your chosen organisation and the cause it supports. Different organisations have different approaches to the use and format of a 'case statement'. A number of American universities, for example, publish their case statement as a formal document – rather like an appeal brochure. The common aspects are an explanation of the importance and relevance of what is being planned, a justification of the organisation's ability to achieve it, and a picture of the resources needed. The best ones combine a sense of immediate need with a self-confident tone so that donors are assured of the positive outcome of their investment. This is helped enormously if the need is set in an external context (hence the reference to looking outside the institution to the wider environment) and engages both the heart and the mind.

The main case statement, whether published externally or not, acts as a container for specific appeals or initiatives which may each have their own case statement, in a way which has parallels with the interlocking levels of planning that organisations use (e.g. strategic, business and operational plans). We hope that you have found this activity useful in beginning to develop an overall case statement on the organisational level which will help animate and unify separate communications in support of distinct appeals or events. The final point about including the donor's role in helping achieve the fundraising goal is a useful pointer towards what we will be studying in Session 2. Keeping your audience in mind at all times is an essential ingredient of effective communication.

1.2.1 The internal function of your case for support

There are a number of key internal benefits of developing your case in this careful way. These are relevant both to you as an individual fundraiser, and to the wider organisation:

It provides you with a personal checklist. Your case document will change over time as you refine and redraft it. At each stage you will be able to identify the information that you already have and what you still need to find out – often from other people in the organisation. The case statement needs to be written or revised in consultation with the most senior levels of your organisation's management. But involving as many colleagues as possible in the process of gathering information will help promote the case statement as an internal focus.

It gives you the basis for sharing information with colleagues. As we have seen, this can strengthen the case itself as well as fuelling productive internal relationships. If you take soundings to check and clarify your message inside the organisation, then there is greater likelihood that your colleagues will feel engaged in the process and will understand what you are trying to achieve.

It will highlight areas where there might be different views or tensions within the organisation. These can surface through things such as the use of language, images or anecdotes. This can not only enrich the emotional/rational balance of the case for support, but also indicate potential ambiguities or problems early enough for them to be corrected in the communications which the case inspires.

It will correct misunderstandings or misinterpretations on your part, making sure that key points are based on evidence and that any facts and figures you use are robust and internally consistent.

If you work in a large organisation, then this sort of internal testing will help you to anticipate difficulties which might lie in wait further down the line. If you work somewhere small, then engaging volunteers and committee members at this stage can also add value. Sharing the case statement internally means that staff and volunteers are kept up to date with the messages the organisation needs to promote.

In any setting it is also helpful to ask one or two people outside the organisation to have a critical look at the case and its presentation. If you are too close to the organisation, its language and its cause, then you can forget that what is obvious to you is far from obvious to people outside – including potential donors.

1.2.2 The external function of your case for support

The case statement's essential function is to equip your organisation to attract support and resources from external donors and funders. It does this in a number of ways:

It forms a sound basis for communication with potential donors, funders and supporters. A well-articulated case statement means that the messages you present to external stakeholders are consistent with each other and with the overall purpose of the organisation. This is particularly true when you are in the position of having to address a number of different audiences, each of whom has separate motivations and interests in what your organisation is doing. A list of such audiences might include groups as diverse as local authorities, company directors, wealthy individuals, and schoolchildren. You will want to address each of these groups with a different kind of message. Maintaining one overall source for each version ensures that the messages do not contradict one another.

It aids accurate understanding of what makes your organisation special. In the next session of this book we will emphasise the need for shared understanding as a basis for communication. A case statement can provide supporters and an organisation with a common purpose and language in this way. Articulating the values and capabilities of your organisation to supporters using appropriate imagery and language helps you to ensure they understand them in a coherent and relevant way. This is one of the reasons why the case statement needs to be shared with volunteers and other workers within the organisation. Because of the highly credible word-of-mouth contact they have with external audiences, their accurate understanding of key messages is essential.

It motivates people to give. As we have seen in the World YWCA example, an effective case is not just a statement of information. It motivates people by drawing on emotional and rational cues, as well as identifying a need that is urgent and deserving of immediate support. Including a time frame in the case statement is a good idea from this point of view. Doing this helps the organisation to couch its aspirations in realistic terms. It also inspires the potential supporter with the thought that the need requires a specific response on his or her part by a certain date.

It shows how donors can make a difference. While a timescale can help dramatise a need by adding a sense of urgency and challenge, it must also be realistic. By presenting a credible and achievable programme, your case statement can inspire the trust of donors and funders. Many organisations include budgets and tables of gifts (opportunities to support the cause at different levels of commitment) in order to facilitate this sense of involvement.

It acts as a container for other cases. For example, a university trying to raise a substantial sum of money in order to resource its development on a number of fronts might have an overall case into which fit a series of smaller case statements, each dealing with a particular aspect of the appeal. Thus the business school will have one message about need, service, case and cost, and the athletics facilities another. While different in their focus and likely appeal, these separate cases will be supported by the overall organisational case with its emphasis on the general effect (for example, of excellence or leadership) which the institution is aiming to achieve as the sum of its efforts.

1.3 BARRIERS TO STATING YOUR CASE EFFECTIVELY

As with any form of communication, devising and writing a case statement is not easy. Getting the level of detail right is one challenge. Too much detail and you risk losing the attention of the reader. Too little (especially if the case statement is about a particular event or initiative) and the statement can become woolly and unconvincing. Another challenge is the matter of language. If you attempt to be over-technical and professional-sounding, the tone can become cold and alienating. At the same time, the case statement is a serious document – so accuracy and correct terminology is essential. As with so many aspects of fundraising, writing case statements is an iterative process – you will find yourself drafting and redrafting as you take on board the results of consultation inside and outside the organisation as the document takes shape. Here are some potential pitfalls to avoid as you put yours together:

Woolliness about purpose or plans. If you want them to respond to your good cause, donors, funders and supporters need to be able to get a clear idea of the purpose of the organisation or initiative advocated by the statement. You might not be in a position to articulate this, because there is still a lack of clarity about the direction the organisation or initiative is taking. Rather than rushing headlong into the market with a vague or premature case statement, time would be better spent working on the issues until they become clear.

Even if the purpose of the organisation is clear, the case statement needs to convey a realistic sense of how this purpose is carried out. An effective case statement will give a clear impression of the strategy the organisation is using to achieve its mission or primary goal, as well as describing the strategy for raising funds to support this. Outline programmes and budgets with appropriate explanations enhance this sense of realistic planning.

Assertions rather than evidence. Rather than making airy assertions your case statement needs to present sufficient detail and evidence to back up the claims you make for your organisation and its work. How you present this evidence is also important. Even something as simple as saying 'One in ten young people' rather than 'Ten per cent of young people' can make your statement more vivid without detracting from its credentials.

Fine detail. As we have already mentioned, getting the level of detail right is a challenge to anyone writing a case statement. Statistics and figures can add solidity to a case – particularly if they are memorable and underline an important point. However, too much detail can obscure the broad lines of the case and its justification.

Forgetting donor motivation. The fundraising cycle (Figure 1.1) places the case statement as the first phase of the cycle, immediately followed by research. One of the topics such research can usefully illuminate is what motivates donors. We all naturally make assumptions about this – and often they are not too far from the truth. But, particularly with case statements for events and initiatives which target a limited range of donors or supporters, such assumptions need verification through research. Later in this book we will be exploring a number of formal research and data-gathering techniques. Understanding donor motivation can draw upon a range of such techniques, as well as less formal opportunities such as meetings, social occasions and networking with donors, funders and supporters.

Language. The use of language is an easy aspect to get wrong, especially in a concise form of communication where every word counts and accuracy is important. Although technical jargon can save time when you are communicating with internal colleagues, its meaning may not be clear to your external audiences.

Emotionalism. It may be tempting to try to exploit the emotions of your potential donors and supporters by becoming sentimental or sensational about your story. However, this has a number of weaknesses as a strategy. First, it demonstrates scant respect for your audience, by underestimating their rational intelligence. Second, it makes it almost impossible for you to stress the unique contribution your organisation or project is making. Emotion tends to swallow up the finer points of detail and reduce everything to the same common denominator. Shock tactics may have their place in certain advertising or promotional contexts, but the case statement is not the right place for them.

As you may have noticed, those six points spell out WAFFLE – always something to avoid when communicating with busy readers.

ACTIVITY 1.3

Briefly evaluate the following fictional case statement based on the above criteria.

COPGROVE CULTURAL CENTRE Case Statement

Mission and Values

The Copgrove Cultural Centre is a joint venture of the North Oakshire County Council, Oakshire County Archives and the Copgrove Local Historical Society. Together these agencies are dedicated to increasing an appreciation and understanding of the story of the border region of Copgrove and Oakshire through collection, preservation and education.

North Oakshire County Council promotes Oakshire arts and artistic endeavours. It collects and preserves a fine-art collection going back to the nineteenth century, including a valuable collection of watercolour landscape paintings. Oakshire County Archives is responsible for the management and care of local government records, and has collections of considerable scholarly interest. The Copgrove Local Historical Society promotes an understanding of the history of the region, maintaining a collection of historical artefacts, early photographs and documents.

Our responsibility to the citizens of Copgrove and Oakshire

A critical responsibility of the Copgrove Cultural Centre (CCC) will be collecting, conserving and making available to scholars the collections of each one of its three constituent agencies. Though these collections have considerable financial value, they have a much greater value in non-monetary terms as irreplaceable cultural resources. Today there are major challenges to preserving the collections and taking full advantage of them as educational, cultural and academic resources. Some are in danger of being damaged beyond repair because of the grossly inadequate storage conditions in which they are held. Difficulty of access to the material has presented their full exploitation by scholars researching the culture of Copgrove and Oakshire.

The current situation

The staffs and collections of the three agencies are currently scattered among no fewer than five different buildings. One of these is due to be demolished as part of the Copgrove Urban Plan. This means that the collection of the Oakshire County Archives must find a new home – and the opportunity of combining this invaluable collection with those of the two other agencies is too good to miss.

Our Vision: An Educational Resource and a Powerhouse of Ideas

The new Copgrove Cultural Centre will house all three agencies and their collections in a specially converted and renovated former school building. This will also provide an attractive venue for a new visitor attraction – the Oakshire Experience, which commemorates over three hundred years of cultural change in this fascinating border region. Using state-of-the-art interpretation and VR technology, the Oakshire Experience will be the first such resource in the country to be fully funded through private-sector sponsorship, donations and entry fees. Oakshire's story is unique. It is a story of change, heroism, resistance and adaptation to change, and post-industrial struggle to form new cultural identities in a constantly shifting world.

The CCC will be a locus of developing new interpretative paradigms for the study and development of ideas about

Oakshire's people, heritage and future. It will be a place where families, schoolchildren, researchers and visitors from outside the region will learn about Oakshire and Copgrove through exhibitions, conferences, workshops, displays and demonstrations, and the very latest in holographic packaged and online media.

Feasibility

A feasibility study conducted on behalf of the trustees of the CCC by management consultants indicates broad support for the cultural centre at local and national level. They identify considerable approval for the establishment of a major financial campaign. The CCC is currently awaiting the outcome of its application for charitable status, but this is likely to be soon. Johann Arbour, the founder and Chief Executive Officer of Copgrove Computing Services, is chairing the board of trustees of this innovative project, whose members are a representative selection of local business people and culture enthusiasts,

Criteria

Wooliness or clarity of purpose?

_____

_____

_____

Assertions or evidence?

_____

_____

_____

Fine or appropriate level of detail?

_____

_____

_____

Forgetting or involving donors?

_____

_____

_____

Language?

_____

_____

_____

Emotionalism?

_____

_____

_____

This sounds like a worthy enough project – and the overall purpose of bringing the collections together into one convenient location is clear. However, there are several aspects of the case statement which need development in the light of the listed criteria. It lapses into jargon on several occasions (for example, the phrases 'locus of developing new interpretative paradigms', 'packaged or online media' and 'state-of-the-art interpretation and VR technology' could do with translation). While the cause is not as emotive as some, the phrase 'grossly inadequate' seems rather strong for its context. With regard to detail, we need more information about timescales and budgets in order to assess how realistic the plans for the Centre are – and a much clearer idea of what will be involved in carrying them out. Claims are made about the value of the collections to be preserved – but they would be far more impressive were they backed up by independent testimony or evidence. Finally, the issue of donor motivation is unclear. There is little here to underline the urgency of the cause, or to mobilise donor motivations based on loyalty to a particular academic or cultural institution or sense of shared heritage.

It is, of course, all too easy to criticise the efforts of others, and it might be objected about this case statement that it is a fictional example set up in order to be knocked down. However, although parts of it have been exaggerated to help illustrate the points made in the text about barriers to effective case statements, it is based – not too distantly – on a real document.

1.4 SUMMARY

Here is a summary of the main learning points from this session:

- A case for support sets out why donors should give to a charity and how donors can contribute to the charity's activities.
- 'Establishing a case for support' is the first stage of the fundraising cycle (followed by 'Research', 'Develop the plan', and 'Monitor and evaluate').
- The fundraising cycle is a version of the planning control loop adapted specifically as a fundraising planning tool. It's a cycle (or loop) because each round of research, planning and

evaluation increases the organisation's ability to establish a compelling case for support.

- Just as there is a hierarchy of strategic, business and organisational levels of planning, so an organisation's overall case for support can provide the framework for case statements for individual projects or appeals.

- Different organisations have different ways of approaching the preparation of a case for support and different names for this document or process, but there are a number of features which effective case statements have in common. These include consistency with donors' values and interests, reference to the wider environment, accuracy, appeal to both heart and mind, urgency and a positive tone.

- The case statement is a valuable internal tool for fundraisers as follows:
  - a personal checklist of issues which may change over time, revealing areas where information needs updating
  - helping share information with colleagues
  - revealing areas of internal tension
  - correcting misunderstandings.

- The case statement's value as an external tool includes:
  - providing a sound basis for communication with external stakeholders
  - underlining the distinctiveness of the organisation
  - motivating giving
  - demonstrating how donors and funders can make a difference
  - ensuring coherence across a fundraising programme with a number of projects and appeals.

- Barriers to effective case statements include:
  - wooliness
  - assertions rather than evidence
  - fine detail
  - forgetting donor motivation
  - language which is overly technical
  - emotionalism rather than a balanced appeal to heart and mind.

Session 2

Introducing Communication

CONTENTS

2.1 Introduction   **31**

2.2 Understanding communication   **32**

2.2.1 A model of the communication process   34

2.2.2 Communication and culture   37

2.3 Defining your audience: segmentation and targeting   **37**

2.3.1 Segmenting your audience   39

2.3.2 The dangers of segmentation   43

2.4 Finding out about your audience: market research   **44**

2.4.1 Secondary and primary data   45

2.4.2 Research techniques   49

2.4.3 Focus groups   50

2.4.4 Surveys   52

2.5 Summary   **57**

2 INTRODUCING COMMUNICATION

2.1 INTRODUCTION

This session begins by looking at the communication process. It presents a model of human communications that will help you understand what is going on when you communicate with other people. Models cannot hope to represent communication in all its complexity, as we will see. But they can help us think about what we are doing when we communicate, in a way which helps us to get key messages across.

Some knowledge of your audience is important for effective communication. The more you know about your audience, the more you can match what you say to your audience's abilities, interests and concerns, and the more you are likely to communicate. Sections 2.3 and 2.4 focus respectively on how you can identify and find out about your organisation's different audiences through segmentation and research.

Aims and learning outcomes

The aims of this session are:

- to present a model of the communication process and introduce a number of important concepts to help explain the problems and issues that are likely to confront you in public relations and communications work
- to explain why knowledge of your audience(s) is important in communicating effectively
- to introduce the concepts of audience segmentation and targeting
- to consider how various market research techniques can be used to find out about your audiences.

After studying this session, you should be able to:

- describe in your own words what happens in communication with reference to a simple model

- explain how getting your message across may be affected by the wider context, especially cultural differences

- analyse your organisation's audiences and segment them into different target groups

- explain the difference between primary and secondary data, and list the main advantages and disadvantages of a number of qualitative and quantitative research techniques

- recognise appropriate occasions to use different research techniques.

2.2 UNDERSTANDING COMMUNICATION

ACTIVITY 2.1

What is happening when you try to communicate with someone? Figure 2.1 is an example of a piece of publicity material put out by a voluntary organisation. It is the front cover of *Visible Voices*, a collection of exemplary projects run by and for young people around the UK. It is one of a number of 'Ideas Annuals' published by a group called Community Links in order to share good practice and inspiration among voluntary organisations. Look at it carefully and then try to answer the following questions.

(a) Who is intended to see this?

_____

_____

(b) What other groups of people are likely to see it?

_____

_____

(c) What is the message that comes over to you?

_____

_____

(d) Do you think it is the message that the writer intended?

_____

_____

Figure 2.1 The front cover of *Visible Voices* (Source: Community Links, 2007)

Visible Voices is a publication intended for people working in community development, but it will also be seen by members of the general public, people in the media, people working for companies or trusts that might fund some of the activities, people making policy in government and elsewhere.

Here are some possible reactions to it: cheap and cheerful; rather messy and amateurish; confusing; fun; happy political correctness; a rose-tinted view of multicultural community action.

> *It is possible that the primary audience will find this rather informal style less intimidating than a more 'professional'-looking document. However, the danger is that others might think the contents will be amateurish, messy or perhaps too good to be true. In fact the document is full of useful ideas, has a good contents page and is attractively laid out.*

In the real world, it is very rare to do what you have just been doing in Activity 2.1 – to concentrate solely on one publication for several minutes and analyse it in the way you have done. Most of the time, people are receiving messages with only half an ear or half an eye.

Even when you are talking to someone you know, face to face, you cannot be sure they are taking in all you say or understanding it in the same way you do. If you are communicating at one remove, perhaps by letter or in a report, you have no chance to check what they are taking in. So the chances of misunderstandings going undetected are higher.

These examples show that communication is not a straightforward process. Sending a message is not a guarantee that it will be received, nor that if it is received it will be understood in the way that you intended. So let us look more closely at what actually goes on in the process of communication that we usually take for granted.

2.2.1 A model of the communication process

Figure 2.2 shows the classic model of the communication process as going from a source, as a message, through a channel to a receiver. It derives from the study of communication as a technical process, where telephone engineers were concerned with the problem of how to transmit a message so that when it was received it approximated as closely as possible to the message sent.

All messages have a *source* or *sender* and a *receiver*. The sender *encodes* the message (for example, into words) and sends it through a *channel* (such as a telephone line) so that it can be *decoded* (in this case, heard) by the receiver. The aim is for the message 'sent' to be the same as the message 'received'. In practice, there will be some *noise*, which will tend to distort the message. Noise may be generated because components in the transmission system do not work perfectly (for example, the crackle on telephone lines), because of mistakes during encoding and decoding or because of outside interference. The loop is completed by feedback from the receiver to the sender. This might be through answering back literally or through doing something which suggests that the message has been received and understood.

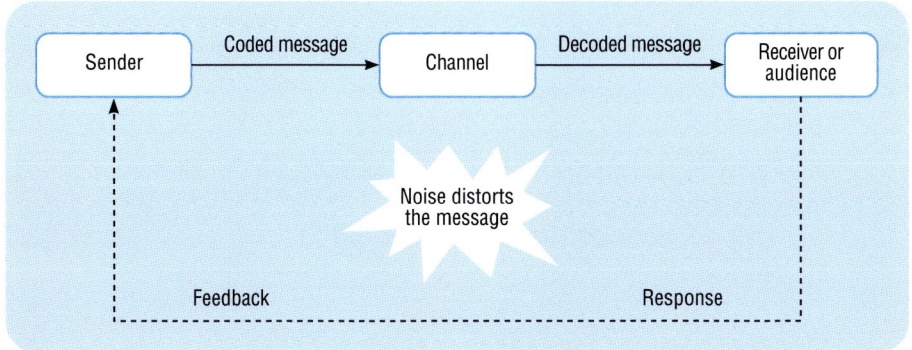

Figure 2.2 The communication process as source, message, channel and receiver

This classic model of communication and the concept of noise are useful in explaining some of the ways in which messages can get distorted. However, such concepts need to be used with care when thinking about human communication. People are not machines: they don't just encode and decode messages; they actively select and interpret them, try to make sense of them, and strive to give expression to their thoughts.

Any message is transmitted via some medium, such as a letter, a telephone call or a newspaper advert. The medium constrains and shapes the message that can be sent. For example, a radio advert means that you can use both words and sounds, but the amount of time you have is very limited, so you can only express a fairly simple message. The medium also gives authority to your message or undermines it. For example, a positive news report on the radio or television about your organisation may add weight to your message.

People don't just passively receive messages: they actively *select*, *filter* and *interpret* them. If people don't think a message is likely to be interesting or important they may ignore it altogether, particularly if, as is usual, it is competing with a variety of other messages. Even once we have decided to concentrate on something, our minds may wander if it is not very interesting or we switch our attention to a new message.

The way people think about and decide to respond to a particular message depends in part on their existing values, beliefs and understanding. This is important to remember if you are trying to persuade people about your cause. Rather than seeking to change their views by a frontal assault on their existing beliefs and attitudes, you will be more effective if you couch your arguments in terms which do not challenge their preconceptions directly.

ACTIVITY 2.2

(a) Think of a recent situation when you misunderstood someone, or someone misunderstood you. Using Figure 2.2 to help you, list some of the reasons why the misunderstanding took place.

_____

_____

_____

_____

_____

(b) How could you have tried to find out whether or not the message had been understood?

_____

_____

_____

_____

_____

(a) There might be a number of reasons for misunderstandings in the communications process. Some, such as distractions or technical problems, we have already dealt with. Others might include emotion or prejudice on the part of sender or receiver, lack of time or attention to what the model calls encoding or decoding, or using language or images which are inappropriate or ambiguous. Channel choice is another important issue. There are some things you would not want to deal with on the telephone, for example.

(b) How did you get on with the second question? One of the most persistent barriers to effective communication is the belief that we have been understood when, often, we haven't. Ways of checking understanding in face-to-face or telephone communication include looking or listening for clues such as facial or verbal expression, body language and eye contact. Questions and summaries can be useful, too. It is much more difficult to ensure understanding in impersonal communication (for example, using advertising or a press release). Trying out ideas on colleagues, particularly those to whom the message is unfamiliar, is a good precaution.

2.2.2 Communication and culture

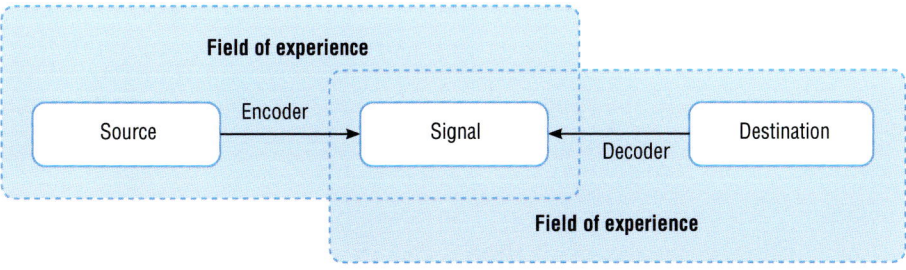

Figure 2.3 Communication as shared experience (Schramm, 1954)

The basic model of the communication process illustrated earlier at Figure 2.2 has been built on by later researchers. Some emphasised the need for senders and receivers to have something in common – an overlap in their fields of experience. Figure 2.3 explains effective communication in terms of this overlap – a shared language, for example, or the fact that we have lived through a particular experience in common. In fact the whole cultural framework in which we and our audiences live affects the way the message is both sent and interpreted. The cultural significance of words and images and the different meanings that can be attached to them have been highlighted in recent years by emphasis on inclusive language (what its critics often refer to as being 'politically correct'). Words and images that some groups might find quite normal and acceptable are felt by others to be degrading or to reinforce negative stereotypes.

In most societies, there is a dominant culture which tends to take its own frame of reference as 'given'. In the UK it is often argued that the dominant culture is southern, white, male, middle class and middle income. Many people doing this course will be involved in organisations in the UK or elsewhere which would consider themselves to be outside the dominant culture, peripheral to or even opposed to it. Other readers will be members of the dominant culture, though the people they are seeking to communicate with may not be.

Communication between different groups with different cultural backgrounds is often problematic, and the first response can be to throw up your hands in the air and declare 'It's all too difficult. I can't say anything right.' Understandable though that is, it doesn't get you very far. There are no easy answers. However, a recognition that cultural differences exist and are important, and a willingness to explore them, are significant steps towards understanding your audience's perspective.

2.3 DEFINING YOUR AUDIENCE: SEGMENTATION AND TARGETING

As you saw in the last section, if you are to communicate effectively you need to know your target audience(s). Who are they? Are they aware of you? What do they know about your organisation and what do they think of it? What is likely to attract their attention and interest? The first stage in the process is to try to be clear who your audiences are. The more precisely you can define your audience and the different segments or sections of it, the more you will be able to target your message to their particular interests and needs.

Public relations consultants talk not of audiences but of 'publics'. Journalists working in different media describe them as 'readers', 'listeners', 'viewers', and so on. For convenience, we are using the word 'audience' to cover all these, and to mean simply the people who receive your message, and 'target audience' to mean those at whom you are aiming it.

Another way of thinking about your audiences is as a range of stakeholders: persons or groups with a legitimate interest in your organisation and what it does, and the capacity to affect it. It is essential to identify your most important stakeholders as key audiences and keep your lines of communication open to them. Figure 2.4 shows a stakeholder diagram for a typical local branch of a national charity providing services for elderly people. Like any organisation it has employees, managers, suppliers, people and organisations to whom it supplies services, neighbours, competitors, and so on. Later in the session you will have the opportunity to draw a similar diagram for your own organisation in order to help you think about your communication priorities.

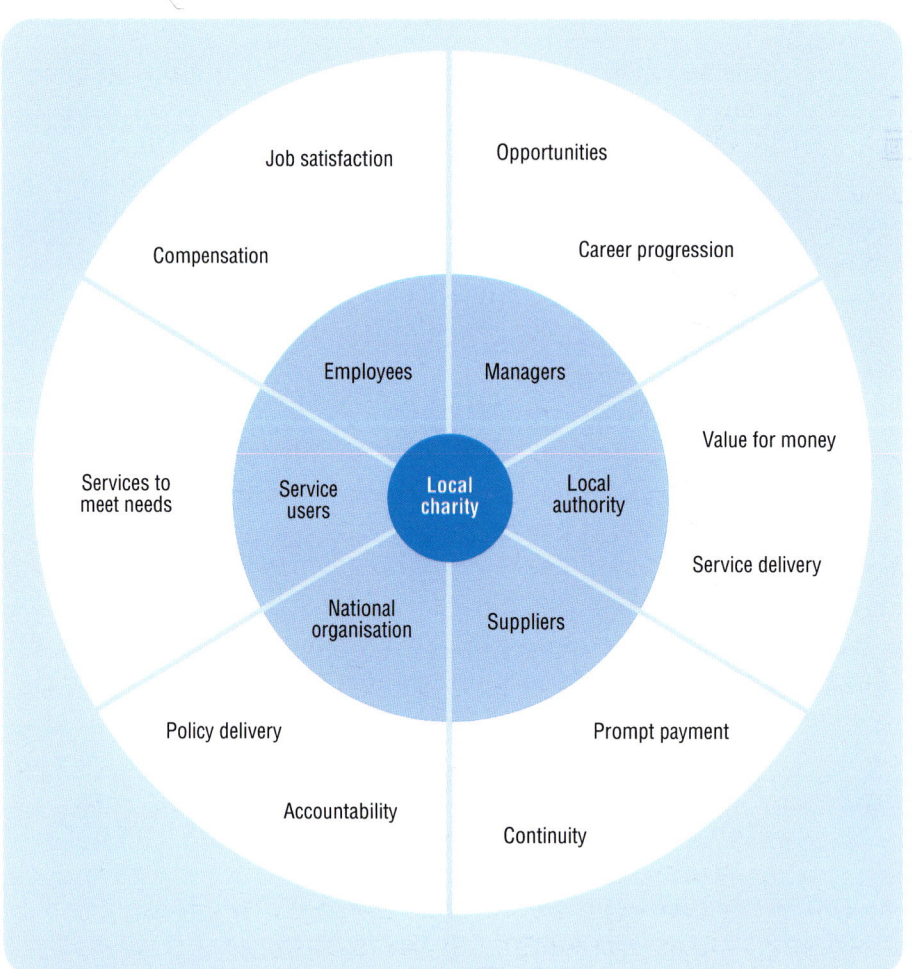

Figure 2.4   Stakeholders and their expectations

Most organisations have a number of audiences who require different communications approaches – potential and actual donors, grant-making trusts, local and national policy makers to name just a few. Your staff are one of the most important. If they are informed and motivated about what your organisation is trying to do they are likely to be much more effective. This is particularly important in larger organisations, or ones operating from several sites, where more informal means of communication often break down.

2.3.1 Segmenting your audience

Segmentation is one of the most useful ideas that marketing has to offer to organisations and individuals engaged in winning resources and support. People's purchasing decisions (which include their decisions about if and how to spend their time volunteering and which causes they are willing to back) tend to reflect characteristics they have in common with other people. So, for example, the kind of holiday you take will depend on your age, the number of children you have (if any) and your interests and hobbies. Rather than just offering the same holiday experience to everyone, travel agents and tour firms have identified important segments of the holiday market and developed a range of different holidays to cater for them. This process is called market segmentation and has been described as: 'the process of splitting customers, or potential customers, within a market into different groups, or segments, within which customers have the same, or similar requirements satisfied by a distinct marketing mix' (McDonald and Dunbar, 2004). A distinct marketing mix will cover the precise nature of the product or service being offered, how much it costs, how it is made available and – crucially – how it is communicated. The effectiveness of your fundraising will be multiplied by a similar approach.

The advantages of segmentation include:

- increasing organisational effectiveness by focusing on particular donor types and motivations rather than squandering resources on people who will not be interested

- attracting a particular group of donors by tailoring your approach more appropriately than rival organisations

- helping organisational planning by learning about, and predicting, the needs of key groups.

In order to make the best use of its time and efforts, an organisation seeking support from different possible sources needs to prioritise potential segments for communication. The most promising segments will be big enough to repay the effort and cost involved, have a clear identity which makes it easy to track and measure their behaviour, have a stake in the work of the organisation and be relatively easy to reach. One of the problems about recruiting younger donors, for example, is that they are notoriously difficult to establish regular communications with because of their mobility.

A number of variables can be used to group customers. In our earlier example of holidays the relevant variables were age, family size and lifestyle. Table 2.1 brings together a comprehensive list of the more commonly used variables. They are frequently used in combination to describe actual or potential market segments.

Table 2.1	Some segmentation variables	
Variable	**Examples**	**Possible categories**
Psychographic: the psychological or sociological make-up of supporters	Personality factors Lifestyle	Ambitious Compulsive Green Upwardly mobile
Demographic: the characteristics of supporters which you can discover from census statistics	Age Generation Family life stage Family size Gender	20–35 etc. Baby boomers Married, no children 1–2, 3+, etc. Male, female
Geographic: where supporters live, work or offer support	Country City size Density	Scotland, France, etc. Population: urban, rural
Behavioural: what supporters actually do and their attitude to your cause or organisation	Occasions Benefits sought	Regular, Christmas recognition
(Source: Kotler and Armstrong, 2008)		

Of these four, behavioural segmentation is probably the most widely used in commercial marketing. Confectionery manufacturers refer, all too literally, to 'heavy users' to differentiate them from those who eat only the occasional sweet or bar of chocolate. Charities and voluntary organisations can benefit from segmenting their supporters along similar lines. Figure 2.5 depicts supporters as a pyramid, with potential supporters at the bottom, working through a succession of layers of loyalty to the most loyal and energetic 'leaders' at the top – people who can actually take the initiative in community fundraising. While still drawing on a common case statement, the messages which you would send to potential or casual supporters are different from those directed at regular and active supporters. The latter might be interested in more information about committed giving schemes, or even volunteering opportunities. Potential or casual supporters, on the other hand, might need more relationship-building communications focusing on the urgency of the need your organisation is addressing, and its effectiveness in doing so. The aim is to try and move supporters as far up the pyramid as their circumstances allow.

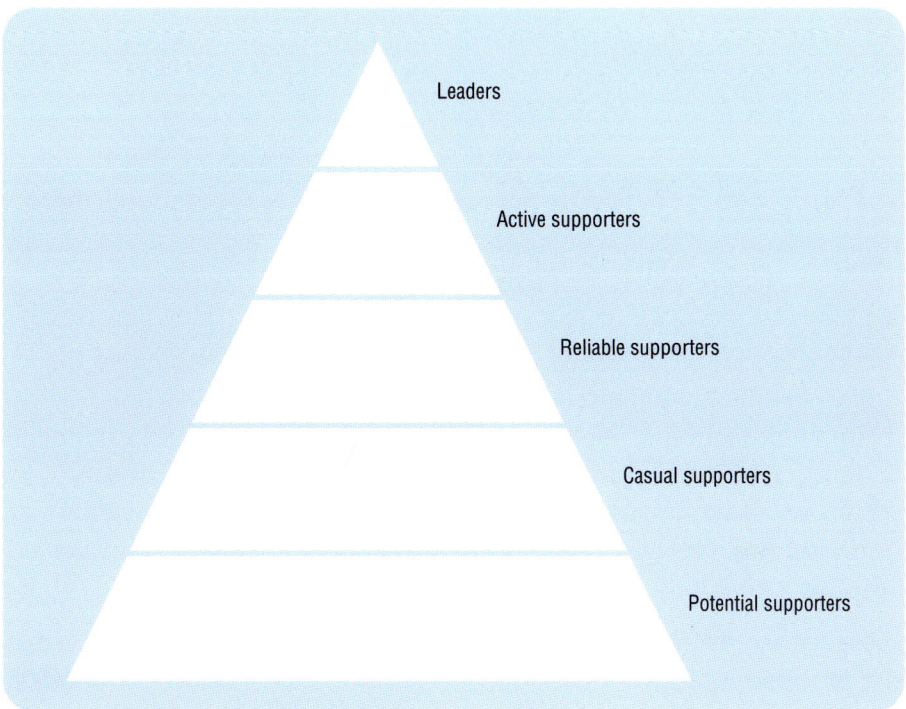

Figure 2.5   The supporter pyramid

In spite of the logic of this approach to segmentation and targeting key audiences with separate messages, there is evidence that many charities and voluntary audiences are much more 'broad brush' in their approach, as seen in Box 2.1.

BOX 2.1

SEGMENTATION SHY?

Researchers at South Missouri State University discovered very broad notions of market segments and target audiences in a survey of Public Relations managers in 21 voluntary organisations. When asked who their targeted publics were, typical responses included:

'the entire community'

'the entire population'

'our targeted audience is everyone'

'pretty much everyone'

The researchers put this down to what they termed a 'public information model' of communication, which conceived of the organisation as a kind of beacon, beaming information about itself out to a general public. While laudable in many ways, this 'one way' blanket model of communication neglects the particular importance of donors or volunteers as groups worthy of special attention. It is important, certainly, to cultivate widespread approval of your organisation's activities throughout the community – but a more concentrated focus of time and effort on the precise sources of support helps use scarce communication resources to best effect.

(Source: Dyer et al., 2002)

Planning segmentation with a diagram can help clarify your thinking about what and how to communicate, and which of the many potential segments of your audience take priority. For example, a cathedral needing to raise money to repair and maintain its fabric might have a number of potential stakeholder groups within its audience, as shown in Figure 2.6, who can be segmented behaviourally on the basis of benefits sought from their association with the cathedral.

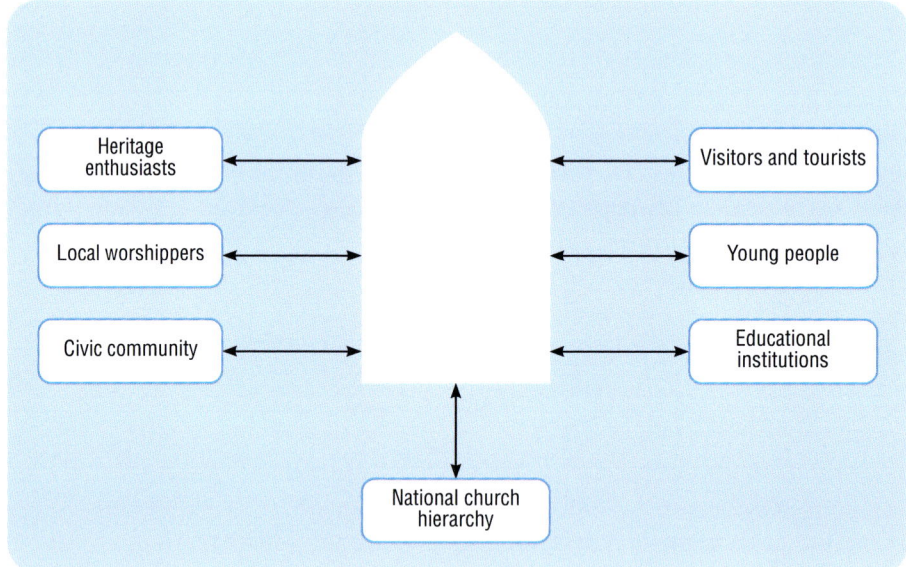

Figure 2.6 The stakeholders for a cathedral

Here, the appeal to people who are interested in local heritage will be different from the appeal to those with a religious commitment to the cathedral, and different again from those who see it as a visitor attraction. Of course, some people will be in more than one of these segments, but the important principle is to prioritise the groups in terms of their value and potential to your good cause, and invest in communicating with them accordingly. As we have seen, commercial marketers have developed a variety of ways of segmenting different groups of consumers using different variables, including geography, demographic characteristics, attitude, lifestyle and behaviour. So, for example, the cathedral fundraiser might notice that heritage enthusiasts had certain of these characteristics in common – perhaps they live in certain sorts of areas, or are similar in age and outlook. This would lead to a more informed approach to targeting potential donors and developing relationships with existing ones.

ACTIVITY 2.3

Try now to draw your own diagram of the audiences for your unit or organisation. Subdivide it into the different groups you want to influence through communication. Segment these groups into other smaller, more manageable categories. Add to each group name a note of the reason for wanting to reach them.

You might like to discuss your diagram with a colleague in due course, or better still get them to do the activity and compare notes. Do they see your unit's or organisation's audiences in the same way? Explore any differences that emerge. In the light of these discussions you might want to alter your diagram.

2.3.2 The dangers of segmentation

Segmentation is not without its dangers, however. Here is a checklist of some of the possible pitfalls to avoid:

- **Too narrow a focus**. One mistake that many organisations have made at times is to concentrate on only one of their target audiences, leaving the others with no message. This can make these groups feel unwanted and excluded, leading to wasted opportunities for support, and even defection to other causes.

- **Assuming that each target audience lives in its own little box**. In reality, the picture is far more flexible and complex. The same individual may be a member of overlapping segments or of different segments at different periods of his or her life.

- **Oversimplification**. It is important to realise that your audiences are made up of individuals who defy easy categorisation – so while segmentation may offer you a guide to approaching them systematically, it needs to be used, like any model, with caution.

- **Getting stuck in a rut**. Effective communication reaches those you want to reach at the time without alienating or excluding those you might want to influence in the future, or in a wider sense.

ACTIVITY 2.4

Look again at the diagram of target audiences you drew in Activity 2.3. Are there any audiences who you think are relatively neglected? If so, what do you think are the reasons for this, and what implications does it hold?

_____

_____

_____

_____

_____

2.4 FINDING OUT ABOUT YOUR AUDIENCE: MARKET RESEARCH

If you are going to communicate effectively with your audience you need to know what their interests and concerns are. As we have seen, 'Research' is the second stage of the fundraising cycle and marks the importance of discovering the motivations and capabilities of donors and other funders in the process of an appeal. A systematic approach to gathering information is thus a key skill for fundraisers and has many uses and forms. Research will identify the individuals, companies and foundations most likely to respond to an appeal. It is also a way of monitoring and evaluating activities, such as communication, to ensure their effectiveness.

In this section we will look at various forms of seeking information under the general heading of market research. Market research is the systematic gathering and analysis of data to help solve marketing problems, in this case applied to fundraising. It is important to stress that market research can become a highly technical subject, and that this is only a brief introduction to it. The purpose of this section is to give you an overview of the main issues. You should either seek expert advice or carry out further study before embarking on any major survey activity.

As Box 2.2 suggests, while research can have an immediate pay-off, many charities are still wary of committing the necessary time and resources.

BOX 2.2

RELUCTANT RESEARCHERS

In 2001 the American charity Food for the Hungry spent $15,000 on a telephone survey of actual and potential donors. The information from the 500 respondents revealed an interesting trend – almost half of them claimed to listen to Christian radio stations several times a week. Matthew Panos, the organisation's vice-president of ministry partnerships, immediately persuaded the charity to divert $50,000 which it had previously budgeted elsewhere to a specialised advertising campaign focusing on such outlets. The result for the year showed a $500,000 rise in private donations over the previous twelve months, which Panos attributed directly to the radio promotion.

Not all market research by charities yields such dramatic results, although charities point to its usefulness in re-engaging lapsed donors, learning what issues and topics donors consider important, and finding out how well their organisations rate against other charities. Organisations that avoid research tend to point towards cost as a major reason for not commissioning surveys (with an average price tag of $25,000 in 2001) and the sheer time spent preparing a survey and analysing its results.

A typical survey takes between 15 and 25 minutes of a respondent's time and can be conducted by telephone, postal questionnaire or, increasingly, the internet. Survey experts point to telephone surveys, which typically receive responses from half of those called, as the most cost-effective and least unpopular method for charitable groups. Internet surveys are a growth area – constituting 40% of the $10 million in surveys which Harris Interactive, a leading US consultancy, did for its non-profit clients in 2001. At approximately one third the cost of telephone surveys, internet surveys can yield useful results – such as demographic profiles of website visitors.

(Source: Wolverton, 2002)

2.4.1 Secondary and primary data

Data is defined simply as raw, undigested facts. An example of data is the number of people using a tax-effective giving scheme (such as Gift Aid in the UK) in order to support good causes. Information, on the other hand, is data that has been made sense of, generally by combining and comparing it with other data. For example, by comparing users of tax-effective giving schemes with other types of supporter, we may discern a trend in their age or income which will help us target further donors in this category.

Market research such as this can be considered as an information management process or system which Dibb et al. (2005) describe in three stages:

1 the gathering of inputs (data) from internal and external sources
2 the processing of the data into information: classifying, storing, indexing and retrieving it (this can be informal as well as formal)
3 the output of informed decision making.

Figure 2.7 shows this diagrammatically:

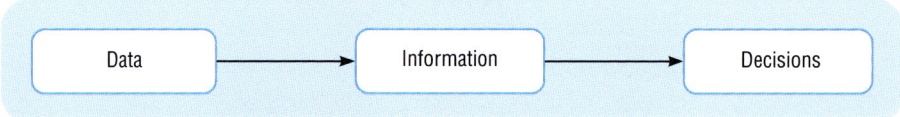

Figure 2.7   An information management system

The data that organisations gather falls into two main categories. 'Primary data' is collected specifically to aid in making a decision (for example to test out a new advertising campaign); whereas 'secondary data' has already been gathered elsewhere for another purpose (for example census data about the age profile of a particular area which might help you target a leaflet drop). Obtaining secondary data is often called 'desk' or 'library' research and is likely to be easier (and cheaper) than obtaining primary data. Yet primary data is what most people envisage when they think of market research (and may well be important in evaluating your communications with specific audiences). However, it is worth starting any market research enquiry with a consideration of secondary data, just in case the information you are seeking already exists.

Secondary data

There are two general sources of secondary data. The first is internal data, for example from your organisation's own records, that is routinely collected. Box office data in a theatre or concert hall would be a good example of this. The second source of data is external – data collected by other organisations either for their own use or for sale. An example of this might be arts or sports sponsorship statistics collected by governments or industry bodies.

ACTIVITY 2.5

(a) Think of three sources of data in your organisation that you could access quite easily and that might provide useful market research information.

(b) Now think of a further three sources of data that exist in your organisation which you do not have access to, but which might provide useful market research information.

You may have found more than three sources of data you could access easily, or found it difficult to think of a further three sources. However, many organisations and managers do not make use of even the most accessible data available to them. Of course, not all accessible data is valuable, but it's worth thinking about what data is available, as this could lead to better and more donor-friendly decisions and interventions in your organisation.

External secondary data comes from six general sources:

Computerised databases. CD-ROMs and online information services can provide rapid access to information at the touch of a button, but can be confusing to the infrequent user. The internet is a vast potential source of information, but presents the problem of information overload (as well as having a great deal of material which has no guarantee of accuracy). Finding exactly what you want from the vast amount of data available takes time and skill with search engines. A critical attitude to sources is necessary, although the voluntary sector and government agencies alike recognise the value of the internet as a place to make information available.

Associations. Almost every business, service or charity belongs to some kind of trade association which, as part of its normal activities, keeps records. For example, the UK's Charity Commission provides consolidated information about donations in England and Wales, or the Charities Aid Foundation (CAF) provides annual reports on giving trends (see www.cafonline.org.uk).

Government agencies. Government agencies – local, national and international – produce demographic data, sales data, employment and import/export statistics, and special reports on particular industries and markets – much of it on the internet.

Published reports. Market research agencies prepare and sell information on almost every conceivable topic. A wide variety of sources is available, but a good starting point in the UK is the Market Research Society's *Annual Handbook*, available in most major libraries. Equivalent bodies in other countries can provide equivalent local information.

Libraries. Librarians are professional specialists in the retrieval of information and can help you find what you need, on paper or electronically. Many libraries offer inter-library loan services and data on grant-giving trusts and corporate donors.

The media. General newspapers, magazines and specialist trade press are a rich source of information. The voluntary sector, in common with other 'industries', has its own collection of such publications – useful for managers to keep up with developments in the sector.

When using secondary data, be careful to evaluate the source and purpose for which it has been collected. This will help determine its relevance to your questions. Furthermore, remember that the basis on which it is collected may vary from one source to another, making direct comparisons difficult. This is a problem, for example, when comparing arts funding in different countries. Not only does the precise definition of what activities are covered by 'the arts' vary from country to country, but so does the balance between direct government subsidy and indirect subsidy through tax incentives to individual givers.

Primary data

Gathering primary data is a skilled process, and many organisations contract specialist market research agencies to do it on their behalf. It is important that, even if you are a non-specialist, you understand the questions to be asked and how the resulting information fits into planning and operations. We will explore some of the main primary research techniques in the next section. First, however, here are three main sources of primary data:

Syndicated research. Rather than commissioning primary research as an individual organisation, subscribers to syndicated research club together to share the costs. Examples of such projects include the TGI (Target Group Index), a long-standing survey conducted by the BMRB (British Market Research Bureau) on behalf of a number of clients, including (in recent years) the Arts Council of England. In an in-depth questionnaire, respondents are asked about their demographics, attitudes and use of products and services in nineteen different categories including media consumption. The results can be cross-tabulated to give a picture of wider consumption habits.

Panel research. This is a form of continuous market research where the same collection of respondents (chosen for their representativeness of the market as a whole) is asked a series of questions over time. A good example of this is the UK's television research (known as BARB, the Broadcasters' Audience Research Board), which tracks the nation's viewing habits by means of a sample of households equipped with 'people meters'. These electric devices indicate when someone is in the room with the television on. By comparing this data with the automatic logging of what channel is playing, estimates of national television audiences can be built up. Programmes succeed and fail on the back of these figures, and buyers and sellers of advertising use the information to bargain about the price of airtime.

Custom research. This is the staple of the market research industry. A specialist agency is commissioned by the client to undertake a specific piece of research. The research company then accepts responsibility for all aspects of the process. There are companies which offer research services across a wide range of fields, and there are others which specialise in particular sectors or techniques. Their projects are usually short term, to answer a specific question. As a result such research is frequently referred to as 'ad hoc'.

2.4.2 Research techniques

A variety of different research techniques can be used to find out about your audiences and their reactions to your organisation. Broadly speaking, research techniques can be divided into two sorts: *qualitative* and *quantitative*. Qualitative techniques are of most use when you want to discover those aspects of people's views, opinions and beliefs that are hard to quantify. Because they don't impose a rigid structure on the respondents, and they allow the researcher to probe and explore the respondents' answers, they are more able to get at people's true feelings and reactions. The most common ways of gathering qualitative data are interviews and group discussions.

In contrast, quantitative techniques are based on the premise that human attitudes, opinions, behaviour and the like can be categorised or measured and thus compared. It is also assumed that the respondents' answers can be meaningfully analysed using statistical techniques to derive results in which you can have a measurable degree of confidence. The most common forms of quantitative research are surveys and tests or experiments. Quantitative techniques are most useful when you want to know things that can readily be quantified, and you want to be able to generalise about your particular audience or the population as a whole.

In discussing these techniques our aim is to help you gain a better understanding of when it is appropriate to use the different techniques and their relative advantages and disadvantages. We do not expect you to be competent to use the techniques yourself after studying this section. There is much more to learn, for example concerning sampling and statistical techniques, and question and questionnaire design. You may also be able to obtain help from contacts in advertising, marketing, or the academic world, either as voluntary assistance or through buying it in. Such consultancy work can be expensive, but if it makes your communications more relevant it can more than pay for itself.

2.4.3 Focus groups

Focus groups are small groups, with usually between five and twelve members, chosen to represent a particular segment of your audience (or market). It is usual to run a number of groups, each representing different segments. Each group is led in a discussion by a skilled moderator on the topics on which you want to find out the range of a group's views and opinions. The moderator's main job is to facilitate the discussion, ensuring that it is not dominated by particular individuals. The discussions are recorded on audio- or videotape. A transcript of each discussion may be made. What people said in discussion is analysed by the moderator and key points are drawn out, which serve as the basis for a report.

Focus groups are useful in getting audience reaction to new communications. For example, you might want to get reactions to a new name, logo, or advertising material. Box 2.3 gives an example of how focus groups have been used by one organisation.

BOX 2.3

THE LISTENING STATION

In the USA, National Public Radio is popular with well-educated, socially-aware listeners. However, the fact that the radio stations in question do not carry advertising means that fundraising is important to them.

Five leading public radio stations funded a study using focus groups to probe listeners' attitudes to fundraising. The groups discussed various stimuli – such as direct mail packages, recordings of telethon-style radio on-air funding drives, and telephone marketing scripts. They confirmed that they made donations to fund public broadcasting because of its importance in their lives.

However, the researchers were taken aback by the strength of feeling against the noisy and frantic on-air fundraising which the stations had been doing up to then. In spite of seeming the most obvious method, it was a big turn-off to otherwise loyal listeners. They hated it for its similarity to the advertising-ridden commercial stations they were avoiding by listening to public radio in the first place. Lottery-type promotions and telephone marketing also got a very negative response. The researchers reported extreme body language by respondents recoiling in horror from a promotional mailing which had been used by one of the participating broadcasters.

Instead, the message from the groups was a strong endorsement of gimmick-free direct mail as a way of soliciting donations.

(Source: Bailey, 2000)

Focus groups have a number of advantages:

- They are relatively quick to organise, and are often cheaper than large-scale surveys.
- Group members are able to give much deeper, richer and better-developed opinions about the topic of research than is usually possible with surveys.
- People often like being asked for their opinion by an organisation they support.

The disadvantages of focus groups are:

- It is difficult to know how representative any group is of the particular audience segment from which it is drawn, so it is hard to know how valid generalisations from the findings are.
- Care needs to be taken so that the moderator's own views don't bias the group – the moderator's main role is to listen and encourage people to talk, not to present their own opinions or justify what the organisation does.
- Group dynamics can affect people's views so that members express opinions they don't usually hold.

ACTIVITY 2.6

(a) Thinking about your organisation, or one that you are familiar with, suggest three topics on which you might get useful data from a focus group.

(b) How else do or might you gather the information on these topics or questions?

An informal way to gather similar information would be to listen carefully to what the audience in question say whenever you get a chance. You might also actively seek out their views, perhaps by asking them for comments, for example on a newsletter. Care would need to be taken not to let your own views influence people's responses.

2.4.4 Surveys

Surveys are a technique in which a sample of the population (in this case the audience you are interested in) is asked questions concerning the issues you are trying to find out about. The sample should be chosen so that it is representative of the people you are interested in.

Questions asked in surveys are most commonly in the form of 'closed' questions. That is, there is some predefined range of possible answers, such as 'yes' and 'no', or some sort of scale (such as choosing a number between 1 and 5 depending on how much you agree with a statement). Some examples of the different types of questions you are likely to find in surveys are given in Box 2.4. The predefined answers mean that individuals' responses can easily be compared. Of course, it is possible to include open-ended questions in surveys, that is, questions where respondents are completely free to make up their own answers. This means, however, that to be statistically useful the resulting answers have to be grouped into categories (a process known as 'coding'). This requires someone to go through the relevant answers and interpret the respondents' often cryptic comments. This may introduce an additional source of error, and is time-consuming and costly. Nevertheless, such open questions can provide valuable information.

BOX 2.4

EXAMPLES OF QUESTIONS INCLUDED IN SURVEYS

A wide range of response formats may be used in questionnaires. Common sense and the need to make any statistical analysis of the results easy are the main consideration on which to base the choice.

In the case of open-ended response questions, you can ask for a reply in either of two ways. For instance:

Overall, what did you like best about tonight's performance? Please write your answer below.

The thing I liked most about tonight's performance was ...

Arguably, the second of these options is better, since by using 'I' it involves the respondent more personally.

Closed-response questions typically involve response options such as 'true/false', 'yes/no/don't know'. Allow scope for the 'don't knows' only if you feel it to be really necessary since otherwise it provides an easy let-out for the respondent who is too lazy to think his/her answers out properly.

To give a broad choice of reply it is advisable to use a closed-response format, but one in which you supply units for the answers. For example:

Approximately how much time did you spend in the gallery today? (tick one)

(a)   Less than an hour ❑

(b)   One to two hours   ❑

(c)   More than two but less than four hours ❑

(d)   Four hours or more ❑

Alternatively, if assessing an attitude or value which cannot easily be quantified, this format might be used:

Please express your strength of agreement or disagreement by circling the appropriate number on the scale.

The Copgrove Players should accept sponsorship from a tobacco company

Strongly agree	1
Agree	2
Neutral	3
Disagree	4
Strongly disagree	5

Finally, at the end of the questionnaire, remember to thank the respondent for his/her help.

(Source: adapted from Hill et al., 2003)

Any survey can only be as good as the questions asked. So they need to be skilfully and carefully developed. There are three important issues to bear in mind when designing survey questions:

- **Bias**. Do the questions allow people to respond in a way which meaningfully reflects their opinions or behaviour, or are they being unduly influenced by your preconceived ideas of what is important? For this reason it is often useful to carry out preliminary qualitative research, perhaps individual interviews or group discussions, in order to establish relevant questions and appropriate response categories.

- **Comprehension**. Will respondents understand the questions in the way that was intended? The use of jargon, unusual vocabulary or complex sentence construction can all lead respondents to misunderstand questions and so give inappropriate answers.

- **Coherence**. Are the questions actually capable of being answered sensibly? Pre-testing questions with a small group of people, similar to those you are going to survey, can help identify problems with language, ambiguity and logic.

Surveys are one of the most common forms of market research. They are often used to get a general sense of how your target audience or population will respond to something. For example, if your organisation produces a donor newsletter or magazine, you might want to carry out periodic readership surveys to help make decisions about how to improve the publication. The survey might look at who reads the publication, the amount of time they spend reading it, the types of articles readers find most interesting, how often people feel that it should be published, and so on. Surveys are also commonly used for campaigning purposes to provide evidence to back up an argument. For example, an environmental organisation might want to find out what proportion of the public in a particular area would be in favour of traffic-calming measures, the hope being that if it did have widespread public support it would add weight to their cause when lobbying politicians. On the other hand, some charities use postal questionnaires which purport to be surveys to raise people's awareness of particular issues and solicit donations. This is disapproved of by the professional marketing research industry and dismissed as 'fundraising under the guise of market research' or 'frugging'.

A variety of different sources of error can creep into surveys. For example, your preconceptions may limit the scope of the questions so that they do not elicit the information you really need; there may be inaccuracies in the way your population is defined; your selected sample may not be representative; the fact that many people do not respond may distort your findings; and so on. So it is usually wise to seek expert advice and guidance when designing surveys, and to test your questions and measures carefully in advance.

In general, the main advantage of surveys over qualitative techniques like focus groups is that they are more likely to give results that are representative of the population as a whole. Box 2.5 illustrates how a major charity uses a regular survey of a representative sample of stakeholders to fulfil its commitment to accountability. However, surveys have the disadvantage that the data gathered often lacks the richness and subtlety that is possible with qualitative techniques. A large-scale survey is more likely to take longer to design, carry out and analyse the results than a focus group. Of course, these techniques are not mutually exclusive and may be used in combination.

BOX 2.5

A QUESTION OF OXFAM

In 1998 Oxfam GB, the UK arm of the international development charity, completed a major strategic review of its activities and direction for the next ten years. One of its recommendations about governance and accountability was the establishment of an annual stakeholder survey to gather information on its performance from the various people and groups with whom Oxfam works in partnership (including staff, volunteers, and project partners). Part of its mission statement says 'Oxfam is accountable both to those who support it and to those whom it seeks to benefit by its efforts', so the stakeholder survey is a way of fulfilling this.

While Oxfam designed the process and questions in the survey, its detailed administration has been carried out by independent consultants, with an overview of the results prepared by a UK academic. Its third year of reporting, 2003/4, revealed the following:

96% of volunteers agree that their contribution makes a difference to the lives of poor people, and 90% feel that their time is well used and appreciated.

Staff report improvements in the organisation's effectiveness at overcoming poverty, in learning and development opportunities, and in cost effectiveness.

Over 80% of supporters are positive about their contribution making a difference and being appreciated.

Areas for improvement are issues in work/life balance in international staff, and a sense from partners in Peru and Serbia that the charity's work could be more relevant and make more of a difference.

The response of the central management team to the report has been to recognise and build on the positive feedback from volunteers, supporters and staff while putting measures in place to address the issues raised about work life/balance and the relevance of projects in the areas flagged.

(Source: Oxfam, 2004a, 2004b)

Surveys can be conducted using self-completion questionnaires sent by post or placed on websites, or by using interviewers to ask respondents questions by telephone or in a personal interview. Some of the main advantages and disadvantages of these different ways of collecting data are summarised in Table 2.2.

Table 2.2 A comparison of different techniques for collecting survey data

Technique	Advantages	Disadvantages
Postal questionnaires	Low cost per person Not obtrusive	Low response level (can be improved by offering an incentive, e.g. entry into a prize draw) Active supporters most likely to respond, hence representativeness uncertain Not good at handling complex questions People often take a long time to respond

Telephone interviews	Good response rate usually Quicker to get response Quite good at handling complex questions	Cost per person higher than for postal questionnaires May be regarded as intrusive Limited use of visual cues Danger of interviewer bias
Internet questionnaires	Low cost per person Can be used over an extended period of time A number of simple packages available Automated data collection and processing	Internet users may be unrepresentative of target audience as a whole Low response level (easy to ignore)
Personal interviews	Good response rate usually Best at handling complex questions	Cost per person usually higher than other techniques Danger of interviewer bias

ACTIVITY 2.7

(a) Thinking of your organisation, or one with which you are familiar, what, if any, topics or issues could you usefully explore with a survey?

_____

_____

_____

(b) What difficulties might you encounter in defining your questions clearly enough to make a survey feasible?

_____

_____

_____

(c) What do you think would be the likely costs and benefits of such a survey?

_____

_____

_____

_____

(d) If you couldn't afford a survey can you think of some other ways you might be able to collect useful information?

_____

_____

_____

_____

The main costs of a piece of research such as a survey are the time and resources needed to carry it out. The likely benefits derive from the fact that the information gathered can help you be more effective. For example, a readership survey may enable you to improve the content and marketing of your publications as a way of enhancing donor relations.

If you can't afford a survey you may be able to gather some relevant information by getting staff to put an agreed set of questions to particular groups when they meet.

2.5 SUMMARY

Here is a summary of the main learning points from this session:

- Human communication is a complex process, prone to error and misunderstanding. Using models to analyse the process can help you plan and carry out more effective communication.

- Two such models are the 'source, message, channel, receiver' model, which breaks communication into discrete stages, and the 'fields of experience' model, which emphasises the importance of shared understanding in communication.

- Segmentation is the process of dividing your audience into groups with similar characteristics and needs in order to address them more effectively. It helps organisations to prioritise and to use resources more economically when dealing with potential and actual supporters.

- Commonly used variables in segmentation include:
  - psychographic (e.g. outlook on life)
  - demographic (e.g. age, gender)
  - geographic (e.g. urban, rural)
  - behavioural (e.g. frequency of donation).

- Segmentation can be dangerous by:
  - taking too narrow a focus
  - assuming segments are mutually exclusive
  - oversimplification
  - getting stuck in a rut.

- Market research is the systematic gathering and analysis of data to help solve marketing problems (here applied to fundraising).
- 'Data' means raw, undigested facts. 'Information' is data which has been made sense of.
- Primary data means data collected for the first time in relation to a particular problem. It can be generated from:
  - syndicated research (joint primary research with other organisations).
  - panel research (continuous surveys of a group of respondents to track trends)
  - custom research (conducted by or on behalf of individual organisations).
- Secondary data means data which already exists, but now applied to a new problem. It can be generated from internal sources (such as donor records) or from the following external sources:
  - computerised databases
  - professional associations
  - government agencies
  - published reports
  - libraries
  - the media.
- Qualitative research aims at understanding respondents' views and beliefs. Common methods are focus groups and interviews.
- Advantages of focus groups include speed, relative economy, depth of information available, enjoyable. Disadvantages include potential non-representativeness, danger of moderator bias and social dynamics distorting individual responses.
- Quantitative research aims at measuring and predicting behaviour. Common methods are surveys (postal, telephone, web and face to face) and tests or experiments.
- Advantages of surveys include statistical rigour and representativeness. Disadvantages include lack of richness of information and specialist skills needed to write, carry out and analyse.

Session 3

Preparing Your Message

CONTENTS

3.1 Introduction   **63**

3.2 Preparing your message   **63**

3.2.1 What do you want to say?   64

3.2.2 Keeping your audience in mind   65

3.2.3 Getting your audience's attention and interest   67

3.2.4 Persuading people to take action   71

3.2.5 Style and image   74

3.2.6 Putting it into words   75

3.3 Summary   **77**

3 PREPARING YOUR MESSAGE

3.1 INTRODUCTION

In the last session you looked at how to identify your different audiences. This session focuses on preparing and delivering your message to a given audience.

Aims and learning outcomes

The main aims are:

- to highlight the key issues to consider in preparing a message: being clear what you want to achieve; anticipating likely audience reactions; attracting your audience's attention and interest; being persuasive and communicating clearly
- to develop understanding of how to prepare and deliver your message to your target audience – taking into account style, image and use of words
- to identify the broad range of possible vehicles for communicating your message, both personal and impersonal
- to develop understanding of how to adopt an appropriate communications mix.

After studying this session you should be able to:

- prepare effective fundraising messages
- demonstrate your understanding of what to say and how to say it to your target audience – taking into account style, image and use of words
- identify and evaluate a range of possible vehicles for communicating your message
- explain the most appropriate communications mix for your message.

3.2 PREPARING YOUR MESSAGE

Compelling messages need careful thought and crafting. What do you want to say and why? How is your audience likely to understand it and respond? How can you get your message noticed and acted on? What are the secrets of clear communication that make the difference between being read and being discarded? This section works through these questions in turn.

3.2.1 What do you want to say?

The obvious place to start when designing any communication is to think about what you are trying to achieve through the basic message you are trying to communicate. As we have seen, your purpose and message are likely to vary between your different target segments. For example, existing donors will usually be interested in what difference their contribution is making, whereas potential donors will need more basic information about the organisation and its work. Of course, it is important to see that there is a reasonable degree of consistency between these messages to present a coherent overall message.

The number of messages you can successfully get across in any one communication is strictly limited. You will be competing for attention with 'noise' created by distractions including other messages. If you try to put over several messages you risk confusing your audience or losing their interest. The medium in which you choose to deliver your message will also affect how much you can say, because of cost or space constraints. Be clear about your main message. It should usually be possible to express this in one or two sentences. As with any communication, you may need to express it in a variety of ways before you can see which will be the most effective and appropriate. Remember that encoding is one of the most challenging stages of the 'source, message, channel, receiver' model of communication.

ACTIVITY 3.1

Thinking of your organisation, or one you are familiar with, consider two different segments that it communicates with regularly, preferably ones that are not too similar (you may find it useful to refer back to some of the earlier in-text activities). Write down one or two sentences summarising the main message to each.

	Segment	Message
1		
2		

3.2.2 Keeping your audience in mind

When preparing any communication it is vital that you keep your audience in mind. Try to put yourself in their shoes. Your message is more likely to be received and understood if it takes into account the interests of the people who receive it. This is where research, even of the most informal kind, can count towards your success. What kind of people are you communicating with, and how can you try to understand them better? According to Kingham and Coe (2005, p. 72) 'There is a need to get inside their minds and understand their lifestyles. Their lifestyles (for example how busy they are, what circles they move in, their personal interests) will affect how they access information and the kinds of messages that resonate with them. There are several ways of making sense of this graphically. One technique used by marketing agencies to understand their customers is to carry out a paper "role play" for the key audiences. Think creatively and imagine how that person gets their information, what they like to read, see or hear, what their interests are then attempt to depict this on paper graphically.' Box 3.1 illustrates this in practice.

BOX 3.1

MEET MR KHAN THE CIVIL SERVANT, MRS JONES THE CONSUMER AND MS WHITING THE FARMER

A group promoting local food (i.e. the principle of viable human-scale farming and marketing to help make local organic food available to all) carried out a paper-based role-play to understand three key audiences who could act as influencers on the Minister for Consumer Affairs. Drawing on their research and understanding they drew up three fictional characters with different personalities, lifestyles, information needs and media preferences. They were then used when planning communications aimed at promoting a change in government policy on local food.

Mr Khan is a senior official in the Department of Trade and Industry. His information comes from trade press, conferences, broadsheet newspapers, academic reports and websites. He prefers information with facts, statistics and models. He is impressed by examples of good practice from local authorities in the area of local food. He can understand and absorb into his work detailed arguments from the group because he is a specialist.

Mrs Jones is a regular supermarket shopper. Her information comes from mid-market newspapers like the *Daily Mail* (a popular paper in the UK) and the radio (both national and local to where she lives). She also enjoys reading gardening and food magazines. She particularly notices stories which have a human element. With a part-time job and young children at home she has not got much time on her hands, so she appreciates simple, practical messages about local food that she can respond to easily (e.g. signing a petition).

Angela Whiting is a farmer and fresh fruit producer unable to get her produce into the supermarkets. She is an active member of a farming organisation, from where she gets much of her information about local food (through briefings and mailings). She watches news programmes on television, but has not got much time to go into complicated arguments. She tends to be most receptive to information which is clearly relevant to her professional interests, and presented in an accessible format (e.g. with visual aids such as graphs). Because she is involved in food production for her living, she can respond to relatively complex demands for support from the group.

(Source: adapted from Kingham and Coe, 2005)

Like the food group in Box 3.1, much of your communication work will be trying to persuade your audience to do something: perhaps volunteer, write a letter to an Member of Parliament or make a donation. So it is important to think through what you can *realistically expect* from different audiences, and to pitch your request accordingly. Objectives for winning resources and support, like any other objectives, can benefit from being made SMART. This popular acronym (a word made up from the initials of other words) stands for:

Specific (the request needs to be clear and capable of being acted upon)

Measurable (a common tactic in approaching a major fundraising task, for example, is to identify target numbers of donations at a number of levels)

Agreed (the request has to fit into a wider strategy which supports the objectives of the organisation or good cause)

Realistic (better to achieve a modest success than a heroic failure), and

Timed (the objective needs to contribute towards a plan with a time-frame).

While for some classes of funder (e.g. grant-making trusts) the amount sought needs to be made clear from the start, this is not always the case. It can be impossible to gauge how much a potential donor might be prepared to give, so the attempt to be measurable and realistic may be based on educated guesswork, and can even run the risk of getting the 'ask' wildly wrong – to the donor's embarrassment or the organisation's disappointment. For this reason it is often a good idea to offer a range of giving levels, depending on the circumstances of the request – a slightly more flexible version of SMART.

ACTIVITY 3.2

Consider the two audiences that you identified in Activity 3.1.

(a) Write two or three sentences about a fictional character from both of the two audiences. Make sure you cover the areas of job, information needs, information sources and likely level of engagement as in the examples in Box 3.1.

_____

_____

_____

_____

_____

_____

_____

_____

(b) What do you think it is realistic to expect from each of these characters in terms of either the size and speed of a donation, or another form of support using the SMART model?

_____

_____

_____

_____

_____

_____

_____

_____

_____

_____

_____

This approach has much in common with the market segmentation process we covered in Session 2. It has the advantage, however, of helping keep sight of the segments with whom you are communicating as a collection of individuals rather than a lumpen mass.

3.2.3 Getting your audience's attention and interest

Any messages that you want to communicate will be competing with a number of distractions. There is a danger that your message will get lost or distorted in this 'noise'. How can you improve the chances that your message will attract people's attention so that they will take the time and effort to read or listen to your message? Box 3.2 contains a number of useful rules of thumb which we hope will make your work stand out from the crowd.

BOX 3.2

CREATING THE OOH! FACTOR

- Think 'YOU': For instance, you hear your own name even in a noisy room. So a new message will be more easily received when it is linked to something which the receiver *knows* about already, and also something in which she or he is interested. Thus a message which is personalised, about 'you' or 'your family', is more likely to catch your attention than one about 'people' or 'families'.

- Think 'NEW': 'Familiarity breeds contempt' and a message that is *too* familiar will be disregarded as 'old hat' or boring. This is one reason why advertisers tend to carry on with successful themes for a long time, but continually refresh the proposition with new treatments of the subject. Another way that you can catch people's attention and avoid overfamiliarity is by an *unexpected twist* or *surprise*. Again this is a technique heavily used in advertising – through the use of humour, pathos or shock tactics.

- Think 'BOO': Sheer loudness or size draws attention, though this might cause irritation, particularly if the place or time is inappropriate. A very loud message has to be very simple as well because we can only take in so much at a time – a poster in large letters might be unmissable but there is only room for it to contain a few words.

- Think 'VIEW': A *strong visual image* is one of the most successful ways of grabbing attention. This is why advertisements include both a picture and words making the same point – the aim is to appeal to your emotion and your reason at the same time. This is even true of radio advertising, where the pictures are created in your mind's eye

- Think 'DO': Asking people to take an *action* also reinforces the message. Once you have filled in a form or made a purchase, you have developed some commitment to the item itself. You are now more likely to recognise its name if you see or hear it again, and, if you then obtained satisfaction, to have built up a favourable preconception. As the saying goes, 'Your best customers are your last customers.'

- Think 'COO': A *positive* message is more likely to be picked up or responded to than a negative, downbeat one. Most of us have problems enough of our own, without needing to add other people's to them. This is quite a challenge for people working to attract support for less glamorous causes, but there is evidence ➡

He'll face 30ft waves, blizzards, force 9 gales and sub-zero temperatures

All we ask of you is £20

- -

To: The Chief Executive, RNLI, FREEPOST BH173, West Quay Road, Poole, Dorset BH15 1XF.

I wish to support the RNLI with:

☐ £20

☐ Another amount £ _____

I wish to give my support by:

☐ Cheque Please make payable to the Royal National Lifeboat Institution

OR ☐ Mastercard ☐ Visa ☐ Maestro

Credit card number/Maestro number   Maestro only

☐☐☐☐ ☐☐☐☐ ☐☐☐☐ ☐☐☐☐ ☐☐☐

☐☐/☐☐   ☐☐/☐☐   ☐☐

Start date   Expiry date   Maestro issue no.

giftaid it ☑

☐ Tick here to increase the value of this donation and all future donations by almost a third through Gift Aid. For every pound you give us we get an extra 28 pence from the Inland Revenue. To qualify for Gift Aid what you pay in income tax or capital gains tax must be at least equal to the amount we will claim on your donation in the tax year.

Name of taxpayer _____
(Only one taxpayer can claim.)

Date _____ / _____ / _____

PLEASE TURN OVER AND COMPLETE THE OTHER SIDE

rnli.org.uk
Charity registered in England, Scotland and the Republic of Ireland.

Lifeboats

Figure 3.1   Advertisement for a charity

that donors exposed to positive messages are statistically more inclined to be generous (Sargeant, 1999). The key is to show how the donor is making a difference. You need to stress what benefits or achievements will arise from their act of support. This is especially the case when an organisation is asking for support over a period of time.

It is also useful to think through the process that people will go through when they receive any communication. For example, if a piece of direct mail is to be successful the receiver will need to pick up the envelope, open it, take out the letter, read the letter, read accompanying material, respond to the request for support. These are all creative opportunities to engage the receiver (through design, graphics, colour, texture) or, if you are not careful, to lose them.

ACTIVITY 3.3

Look at the advertisement in Figure 3.1 and then note down examples of where you can see the use of the rules of thumb described in Box 3.2.

'YOU'

'NEW'

'BOO'

'VIEW'

'DO'

'COO'

It certainly puts the reader on the spot with a direct appeal to 'YOU'. It's 'NEW' insofar as these are facts that might be new to the reader. The reported size of the waves creates a 'BOO' effect, and the visual impact of the photograph is impressive ('VIEW'). There is a clear call to action ('DO'), and the ad invites the respondent to feel part of a heroic endeavour ('COO').

3.2.4 Persuading people to take action

Turning communication into response is helped by three invaluable tools: AIDA, stressing 'benefits not 'features' and 'the call to action'

AIDA

In much fundraising and promotional work you are trying to raise awareness of a problem or an issue, get people interested in your cause, show them a reason why they should get involved and finally persuade them to take some action as a result. This might be to become a member of your organisation, a volunteer or a donor. There is an acronym used commonly in advertising, public relations and marketing to describe this process: 'AIDA'. It stands for Attention, Interest, Desire and Action:

- **Attention**: to get someone to do something you have to stimulate their attention to your message in the first place. An arresting image, an intriguing question, even something that might shock, are all tactics that have worked for fundraisers in the past. What can you think of to make *your* message stand out?

- **Interest**: this is where understanding your audience comes into play. They need to be able to relate to your message in order to be interested in it.

- **Desire**: remember that a fundraising case has to appeal to the head and the heart. Desire is the emotional side of the appeal, a hook or an 'angle' (as journalists call it) which draws the individual in and prompts him or her to think 'yes, I can do something about this and I will'

- **Action**: completing the sequence means indicating a clear course of action which the message recipient can do there and then. Examples include filling out a coupon, visiting a website, phoning a number, writing to an MP, signing a petition, making a donation or pledge of support.

AIDA can be applied to a wide range of communication activities – from an appeal letter to a public meeting. Use it as a checklist the next time you have to prepare or comment on a piece of promotional material, but remember that (like any model) its value is as a tool rather than a straitjacket.

Sell benefits not features

This is yet another useful idea we can take from marketing. Detergent marketers all understand that people do not buy detergent because they want detergent. What they want is clean clothes – and if there was a more convenient alternative than having to wash them they would choose it. In other words, it is the *results* you are offering to achieve, rather than the mechanism by which you achieve them, that will interest your audience. For a cancer research charity, for example, donors are not really interested in the precise details of the medical research they are funding. They want to know that their money and other donated resources are advancing the search for a cure, or at least for an alleviation of the distress associated with the disease. If you are asking for a donation it is a good idea to let people know what it is that will be *achieved* with their money.

Include a call to action

People's time and attention are limited. Having attracted their attention, stimulated their interest and aroused their desire, you need to finish the job by asking them to take action on your behalf. The call to action reflects the urgency of your case statement. The secret is to make it as easy as possible for them to respond so that the sense of urgency is not lost and you get the response you want.

A number of examples illustrate this point. Many press advertisements contain response coupons which are designed to be easy to use (often printed at the corner of the page to facilitate being torn or cut out and returned). Credit cards and the internet mean that telephone numbers and website addresses are just as important as coupons in prompting action by interested respondents.

Whatever the medium used, you can make it even easier for the recipient by indicating the sort of response you want, for example by showing different levels of donation and what can be achieved with each.

When designing your response mechanism, build in monitoring. One useful tactic is to include a code on response coupons so that you can compare the effectiveness of different publications or mailings in attracting replies and learn from your experience of what works.

ACTIVITY 3.4

Write brief notes under the following headings about the advertisement reproduced as Figure 3.1.

(a) How does it:

Attract attention

_____

_____

_____

_____

_____

_____

_____

Engage interest

_____

_____

_____

_____

Stimulate desire

Prompt action

(b) How does it sell benefits not features?

(c) What is the call to action and how is it made?

(a) Attention is attracted by an arresting visual image and a strong headline. A face challenging you to respond with a stare is not exactly a new idea (remember Lord Kitchener?) but works well here. It's even more convincing for being that of a real person whose details appear at the top of the photograph. Representing real people in charity advertising is usually impossible for ethical reasons, but here it strengthens the appeal. Interest and Desire, I think, are run together in the copy – from the heroic feats described in the first headline, to the ironic request for money. Perhaps the emotional appeal here is something like shaming the reader into a response (a very high-risk strategy usually, but this ad gets away with it). Action is very clearly indicated, but could be even more immediately available if there was a 'sign-up' telephone number to save the trouble of finding an envelope, stamp and cheque.

(b) The benefit being sold here is a sense of 'doing your bit' to help heroes – there are no technical details about boats, numbers of rescues or exercises. Interestingly, there isn't even any mention of people being rescued.

(c) The call to action is the whole point of the ad. There are a number of levels of support indicated, as well as the chance to give tax-efficiently and opt out of further contact with the charity. Notice the coding of the coupon in the top right-hand corner to identify where and when it appeared for monitoring purposes.

3.2.5 Style and image

The overall style and layout of any written communication is what readers notice first. If it is attractive and interesting, they are more likely to read what you have to say. Space, attractive typography, photographs and illustrations all contribute to the effectiveness of written communication or the attractiveness of a web page. A picture can be used to attract attention, to add human interest to a story and to reinforce and highlight a particular message. In addition, pictures and illustrations can be used to break up text that might otherwise look monotonous and boring. Using a consistent style will also make it easier for people to recognise your organisation's communications as part of its overall branding.

Image is not just confined to your organisation's personality in print. Professionalism can be communicated in a number of ways. For example, a meeting with a reporter, or a radio interview needs the same level of preparation as a meeting of your management committee or equivalent. A news release or a direct mail letter needs to be drafted and redrafted – remember the lesson from the last session that encoding needs care. And if you are using a communication method such as a discussion face to face or by phone, you need to work out your arguments precisely, and think what the other person may say in return, before you start. Such communication occasions demonstrate the usefulness of having a case statement covering your organisation or its initiatives. The arguments and statistics it contains act as a template which can be adapted to a variety of occasions and allow you to keep 'on message' even when under stress from questioning.

ACTIVITY 3.5

Again looking at Figure 3.1, write brief notes on its style and the image it portrays. Try to summarise the impression it makes on you and the reasons for this.

(a) Style

_____

_____

_____

(b) Image

_____

_____

_____

(a) The style is very direct and confident. Notice that the typeface used is consistent throughout the ad – even though some is in bold and, of course, in different sizes. This gives an impression of coherence. There's plenty of white space also, which adds to the sense of simplicity.

(b) The image is of a straightforward, no-nonsense organisation whose work involves routine acts of heroism. There is an image of documentary realism about the advertisement which complements this – from the details of the lifeboat man pictured to the little flecks of water on his jacket.

3.2.6 Putting it into words

How can you make sure that what you want to communicate will be interpreted and understood in the way that you want by your audiences? In other words, how can you guard against creating unnecessary noise yourself? Box 3.3 lists some more rules of thumb that can help you communicate clearly.

BOX 3.3

BECOME A COMMUNICATION A.R.T.I.S.T.

- Give people an **Action** to take as a result of receiving your message, and make it easy for them to do it.

- Ensure your points **Run** *logically* and that people can see how one arises from another. You may well be taking things for granted because you are so steeped in the issues – but your readers may not be.

- Deal with the **Tangible** rather than the abstract. Give examples that relate to people's everyday life wherever you can. Use the active rather than the passive voice (people doing things rather than things being done by nobody in particular) Refer to homeless people or unemployed people rather than abstract and demeaning categories like 'the homeless' or 'the unemployed'. Let people know what can be achieved with their support.

- Make your message **Independent** and self-contained. Explain as you go along. Give a brief résumé of 'the story so far' when you tell people about the latest developments on an issue. If you use jargon, tell your audience what it means. Don't use acronyms or nicknames without explaining them.

- Keep it **Simple**. Use short words instead of long ones. Get rid of any unnecessary words, break long sentences down into short ones. Avoid complex sentence structures and the use of jargon. This is particularly important when writing for the web. Keep the design and layout of written or visual material straightforward and easy to find a way around. Don't cram too much into any one piece of material.

- Strike a positive **Tone**. For example, refer to 'supporting' your project rather than 'defending' it. Stress what you want to be done, rather than what isn't being done at the moment.

You might feel that to deliberately adapt what may be your normal style in this way is to patronise your audience. But being clear does not mean being patronising. Instead, well-written material shows respect to the reader. No one is entitled to *demand* that others receive and decode their message, but only to *request*. If you make the reception hard work, it will not happen, and your own hard work in preparing the message will be wasted.

It needs more skill to write consistently in a simple and straightforward style than it does to use a style that involves complex words and sentence structures. The seventeenth-century writer Blaise Pascal once apologised to a correspondent 'I have made this letter long because I have not the time to make it shorter' (Pascal, 1997 [1657]). Being both clear and concise is still a challenge to any writer, but becomes easier with practice and is as valuable in the twenty-first century as it was in the seventeenth.

3.3 SUMMARY

Here is a summary of the main learning points from this session:

- Prioritise your messages – the number you can get across in any one communication event is strictly limited.

- Anticipate how your target audience(s) will receive and understand messages through techniques such as a paper role-play.

- SMARTen your communication objectives by targeting Specific, Measurable, Agreed, Realistic and Timed responses from recipients.

- Factors to get your communication noticed include personalisation, surprise, visual images, action, and being upbeat: 'YOU', 'NEW', 'BOO', 'VIEW', 'DO' and 'COO'.

- AIDA stands for Attention, Interest, Desire and Action – a flexible template for communications planning.

- Talk about benefits not features – what's in it for the recipient?

- Include a call to action which is attractive and straightforward.

- In any medium, style and image support effective communication.

- Clear written communication focuses on the desired Action, Runs logically from point to point, emphasises the Tangible, is Independent and self-contained, Simple and positive in Tone: in short, ARTISTic.

Getting Your Message Across

CONTENTS

4.1 Delivering your message   **83**

4.1.1 Impersonal communication   84

4.1.2 Personal communication   100

4.1.3 Personalised communication   103

4.1.4 Deciding your communication mix   107

4.2 Fundraising and campaigning   **109**

4.2.1 Winning political support   109

4.2.2 Evaluating communication   113

4.3 Summary   **114**

4 GETTING YOUR MESSAGE ACROSS

4.1 DELIVERING YOUR MESSAGE

Choosing an appropriate vehicle for delivering your message is fundamental to the success of any communications plan. There are many different possible vehicles of communication. In this section we have organised them into three categories. The first, impersonal communication, offers the opportunity to reach large numbers of people but with minimum adaptation to the needs of each individual. It is one-way in its direction and so it can be hard to gauge response.

The second, personal communication, is the reverse. It involves individual-to-individual contact. This is very powerful, very interactive, and very expensive because of the time involved. However, it is an essential element of much fundraising and campaigning work.

The third category is a hybrid – personalised communication. This uses technology to reproduce some of the aspects of personal communication in a way which allows you to reach large numbers of recipients.

The three categories are summarised in Table 4.1 Choosing the right medium, or combination of media, is key to getting your message to the right people, at the right time, with the minimum of waste along the way.

Table 4.1 Vehicles of communication	
Type	**Vehicle**
Impersonal	Advertising (television, press, radio, cinema, posters) Newsletters Publications (e.g. books, reports, web pages) Media publicity (press releases, press receptions, sponsorship, organisational literature)
Personal	Personal 'selling' and presentations Conferences, events Personal memos, letters, emails and calls
Personalised	Direct mail Telemarketing email SMS (text messaging)

4.1.1. Impersonal communication

Three broad types of impersonal communication vehicle can be defined: advertising, publications, and public relations using the media. Each has its own unique characteristics, and advantages and disadvantages.

Advertising

Advertising is the use of paid-for media to inform and/or persuade potential and existing customers (including, in our case, donors and other supporters). Typically, advertising is designed to reach a mass audience with a direct and simple message. It has a number of uses:

- it has the potential to reach a large number of people, at relatively low cost per person
- it has the potential to affect people's attitudes and behaviour, for example it can be used to recruit new members, get people to come to an event, or solicit donations
- it can increase public awareness of your organisation or cause and the work it is doing
- it can increase the credibility of the organisation
- it can be repeated at different times and in different places.

Advertising is often thought of as an expensive way of getting your message across to people. Indeed, some forms of advertising, such as television commercials and advertising in the national press, do involve high costs and will be beyond the means of many organisations. However, advertising in the local press or radio is often much more affordable; in addition, there is a variety of means of low-cost advertising, for example using leaflets, posters (assuming you can get someone to display them for nothing), swapping advertisements in other people's publications, and so on.

Comparing the real cost of advertising opportunities can be confusing because of this variation in prices. The solution is to work out the cost of reaching the same number of your target audience in each medium (conventionally, 1,000). This is what is known as the 'Cost per Thousand' or CPT. Publications should provide such information, along with details of circulation (how many people buy the publication), readership (the larger figure who actually read it) and the area covered. Similar information is available from broadcasters. Alternatively, you can rely on the advice of a specialist advertising agency, who will not only suggest where to advertise but will also help you with creating the advertisements themselves. Several agencies have charity accounts which they service on reduced terms as a form of corporate social responsibility. Don't forget that it also costs money to produce advertising material (although some publications and broadcasters will include this in the package).

There is also the question of the impact and tone of different media. For example, advertising on television, cinema screens or the internet can all incorporate impressive sound and moving pictures. Radio can be very immediate and intimate. Press advertising can use visual images alongside sufficient words to get across complex messages. It's hard, therefore, to make comparisons between different media unless you take into account what you want your advertising to achieve. The only certainty is that it will cost you money.

On the other hand, you may also be able to obtain the equivalent of free advertising through social action broadcasts (sometimes known as Community Service Announcements); through broadcast appeals, using the letters page of newspapers; or – if you are very fortunate – by getting someone to sponsor your advertisements (as did Microsoft Corporation for the National Society for the Prevention of Cruelty to Children's (NSPCC) award-winning 'Full Stop' campaign).

ACTIVITY 4.1

(a) List in the table below the forms of advertising used by your organisation, or one with which you are familiar. Then, for each specify where the advertisements are placed, which groups they are targeted at and what they are used for. The first line has been filled in as an example.

Form of advertising	Where placed	Target audience	Use
Posters	Shop windows, library, public places	Customers at charity shops, public-minded citizens	Recruit volunteers, increase awareness of organisation and cause

(b) What, if any, methods does your unit or organisation use to assess the effectiveness of these different forms of advertising?

_____

_____

_____

_____

_____

Evaluating advertising effectiveness is notoriously difficult. Most methods involve measuring a proxy for effectiveness, ➡

such as how many people are likely to have seen an advertisement in a particular time period (for example, how many cars or pedestrians pass a poster site per day). For television advertising, panel research determines how many people 'see' ads, but with no guarantees of how much attention they are paying. On the other hand, personalised media such as telemarketing and direct mail, and much internet advertising, allow a direct connection to be made between what a recipient sees or hears, and what they subsequently do as a result.

Publications: print and online

Annual reports, booklets, websites, research reports, newsletters, and leaflets tell people about your organisation and what you do in more detail than with many other forms of communication. On the other hand, it can take considerable time and effort to produce a clearly presented, interesting and authoritative publication. Then there is the job of making sure it reaches the right people in a timely manner.

Other forms of communication are often valuable in promoting and reinforcing the message of your publications. If you have a research report that contains controversial or interesting new findings you might want to publicise it with a press release or news conference. Even short briefing papers can be the subject of a news release if they contain striking statistics or facts. Remember, too, that many of the people you want to read your publications will be very busy. For any document more than a few pages in length it is useful to include a short summary at the beginning. In addition, you may want to offer some guidance to help people find what is most relevant for them. So, for example, if you send a report to a politician who you hope will support your cause, it will help to enclose a covering letter giving them guidance as to which parts they are most likely to be interested in. Keep the AIDA acronym at the back of your mind as you plan your communication.
You need to think very carefully about the implications of committing yourself to a regular publication, such as a newsletter, and make sure that you really do have the resources and time to produce and maintain it with a continuing flow of articles to provide the content. It is no accident that so many newsletters and magazines fizzle out after a few issues. This is also true of websites, where content can age rapidly if not refreshed by regular updates. Box 4.1 contains advice on maintaining a website – but much of what it has to say is relevant to other forms of regular publications (such as the advice about using a style guide to make sure you are consistent in details such as where to use capital letters, or standard spelling. Depending on its size, your organisation may already have such a document).

BOX 4.1

MAINTAINING YOUR SITE

Users expect new and up-to-date information each time they visit your website. They don't care about your resourcing issues. They expect everything to work: no broken links, no missing images, and no typos. You want them to leave the site having had a positive experience and therefore you need a level of dedicated resource. The extent of this clearly depends on the size of your organisation and the resources available to you.

A quick guide to managing your site

Plan a monthly and annual content schedule

Identify key tasks and responsibilities

Write, design and build new content

Establish quality assurance guidelines (see below)

Establish a sign-off process

Planning a content schedule

Identify 'dynamic' content – that is, material which needs to be updated regularly. Think about content areas that you might use:

Micro-content – short headlines and links

News – remember to link to other relevant pages of your site

Campaigns

Fundraising

'Static' content is that which only needs to be updated as and when necessary, such as 'About us' or 'Contact us' sections

Make it readable

When you write, design and build content, it is important to remember that users read about 50 per cent less online. Break up the text using sub-headings and bold text – both make text easier to read. Make sure new content links to old content and vice versa. Keep layouts consistent using templates.

Quality assurance

Users are turned off by spelling mistakes and broken links

Ask someone else to check your work thoroughly

Don't let 'un-checked' work go live

Set an editorial style guide as you would for printed materials

But problems will crop up ...

As content grows, navigation issues occur and you may need to introduce a search facility

The labelling of buttons may become incorrect or inappropriate and will need to be reviewed ➡

Levels of hierarchy may become insufficient

Certain areas may become more popular than others

Old links may become broken

Information may become obsolete or misleading

(Source: Media Trust, 2007b)

The internet has rapidly become a key element in donor and supporter communication for campaigning and fundraising organisations. In spite of intense interest in the potential of internet sites as a new fundraising channel, the early signs are that progress here is likely to be gradual rather than revolutionary (Sargeant and Jay, 2003). On the other hand, providing participants in sponsored events with personalised websites to collect sponsorship from their supporters has considerably reduced the inconvenience of this method of participative fundraising (Grieve, 2005).

Voluntary and community organisations use their websites not only to provide information and documentation, but to sell publications and merchandise, register members and take donations. In fact one of the problems facing website designers is to simplify what is on offer to visitors. There are a number of ways of doing this. One is to make sure that your home page (the first one a visitor sees) includes a site map which shows how the various areas of the entire site are linked together. Another is to promote ease of navigability between sections by clearly available menus. Fundraisers will want to make sure that every screen seen by visitors includes a link to allow them to donate today.

Websites need to try very hard to maintain visitors' interest and prolong their stay. This quality is known as being 'sticky'. Sticky websites offer their visitors value (such as information, interactivity or just ingenuity) in order to encourage participation. Every second that a potential donor or supporter is online to a particular website is a chance to create a dialogue and develop a relationship. Effectively, the internet allows individuals to give an organisation permission to market to them. In order to obtain that permission, the organisation needs to have something worthwhile to say.

Keeping the visitor is one issue, but what about attracting them in the first place? It is important to promote your website at every opportunity on other types of publicity material. It is also important to understand how 'search engines' work. These are sites like Google.com which guide users to information on the internet by offering keyword searches. Such searches typically yield hundreds of pages of potentially relevant 'hits' – only some of which will be of interest. The search engines find out about websites by running software programmes called 'robots' which constantly roam the web, looking for new sites. It might thus be a long time before they find your particular organisation, and when they do, the information they offer a potential visitor in a listing of hits needs to be relevant (as well as sufficiently far up the list to get noticed). This means that a proactive approach to search engines is a good idea. They can be approached either direct or through specialist online registration companies to register your presence. Furthermore, for a fee, many search engines will prioritise a site's position on their listing or offer guaranteed exposure.

ACTIVITY 4.2

Using the points under 'Planning a content schedule' in Box 4.1 as a starting point, briefly review your organisation's website home page (or that of an organisation with which you are familiar). Make brief notes on the following aspects of the page:

(a) the balance between static and dynamic content

(b) interest and relevance of news sections

(c) readability

(d) clarity of links to other pages

(e) fundraising and/or campaigning focus

The home page is the most important part of any website. It needs not only to communicate the essence of the organisation immediately to visitors, but also to offer speedy access to important information or activities (such as making a donation). Getting the balance right between the necessary simplicity to do the former and the sophistication to do the latter is difficult – as you may have noticed from your example.

Working with the media

Advertising and publications give you complete control over your message and how it is put across, but at a considerable financial price. Public relations through the media, on the other hand, let you 'hitch a ride' in print or broadcast news with your message for little or no financial outlay. Don't underestimate the cost in time and creative effort, though. Success in working with journalists is largely a matter of understanding what their objectives are, and how you can work together to mutual advantage.

The long-term aims of any editor or producer can be summed up as:

- survival
- expansion
- profitability.

In the short term, they have to get their product out on time. As deadlines approach this can override almost anything else. They must build their credibility and not be taken for a ride or be manipulated by the vast number of people who (like you) are trying to use them. They want to look good in the eyes of their colleagues and managers. In other words, they are ordinary people doing an ordinary job of work.

Where editors and producers have 'lines', or run crusades, this tends to be less for its own sake than to meet these major aims. Each part of the media aims to cater for different segments of the public. So they concentrate on issues that they believe to be important to their readers, viewers and listeners. They will have found this out partly through market research, but mainly through their editors' own gut reactions and contacts.

There is a tendency to concentrate on a 'flavour of the month' issue for a short time, and then switch to something else. This is partly because journalists are afraid of boring their audience. The reporters can also be bored or find that there is nothing new to say on the issue.

Newsworthiness

Editors and reporters make decisions about which stories to run according to the general heading of newsworthiness, or 'news values'. The first requisite is that news is in fact *new*. The event must be about to happen very soon, be happening now or have just happened, and not be simply a repetition of something that has happened before. Or if it happened some time ago, it needs to have been recently discovered or had some new evidence about it. The urgency of this depends on the publication or programme. For a big city's evening paper, anything that happened yesterday is dead news. For a local weekly, a local event can still be worth reporting even if it happened several weeks ago. For a specialist academic journal, book reviews may appear eighteen months after a book has been published. But with broad exceptions, a rough rule of thumb is that anything that happened before the previous publication date is dead news. Therefore it is important to let the media have details of events *in advance* whenever possible. You can always embargo news releases so that they are not used until the appropriate time (although this irritates journalists unless it is absolutely necessary).

There are techniques for making something new when it has existed for quite some time. Anniversaries, celebrities and stunts are all examples of this. So are landmarks in your work, for example the one hundredth person helped, or the one thousandth new member. Sometimes the same activity can be news several times. If you were to invite a controversial figure to your AGM, for instance, the invitation could be news, so could the AGM itself, and so could reactions to what she or he had said.

The second requisite is that each story must have a clear point whose relevance can quickly be made clear to the audience – a similar idea to the 'angle' we have mentioned earlier. The first paragraph of most newspaper stories summarises this point. So does the almost invariable formula used in news bulletins on TV and radio. This short lead-in tells you whether it is worth reading or listening further to find out the full details. All the rest of the story is an expansion. This lead-in gives not the facts, but the *point* to which the facts relate. Similarly, the first paragraph of any press release should summarise the message you want to put across simply and clearly, and in a way that is relevant to the audience. The editor or producer is aiming for one item, one message, and he or she needs an angle within that, which will interest the readers or the audience.

ACTIVITY 4.3

Think of an activity or event that your organisation or one with which you are familiar might want to publicise.

(a) **What do you think might be newsworthy about the activity or event?**

_____

_____

_____

_____

(b) **What angle(s) could you take on the story?**

_____

_____

_____

_____

_____

_____

For many local papers, the only angle needed is that it is local. For national papers, it might be that something could affect their readers' lives or things they know about – such as a change in taxation laws – or that something is tragic, controversial, scandalous or heart-warming. For specialist journals, it could be the fact that someone has contradicted a leading person in the field or that a new development creates threats or opportunities to their readers' jobs. The same story can have different angles in different places, and at different times.

Creating news

Here are some ways to boost your newsworthiness:

- **Think in pictures**. One of the most familiar and important techniques for creating newsworthiness is with a picture opportunity or a soundbite involving a public figure, a celebrity, or a quickly assimilated image that can illustrate your general point. The more unusual or dramatic the picture opportunity, the more likely you are to gain coverage, as the publicity stunts of organisations like Greenpeace have shown. A good picture will almost guarantee a place in some local newspapers.

- **Come up with controversial facts**. Another common technique is to do a survey. Apart from fulfilling the basic criteria of news (that it is new), announcing the results of a survey gives local media something to bite on if it has local relevance. As a general rule, any survey, or story for that matter, will be more newsworthy if it is *controversial* in some way – for example, if it contradicts conventional wisdom or challenges official policies.

- **Make it personal**. In order to demonstrate the angle and to get the point across to the audience, most news stories involve humans or animals. If they can be named and photographed, and, in the case of people, can make brief comments, so much the better. Where this cannot be done, a story is often 'humanised', by quoting people who are well known or in positions of some authority, or otherwise appealing. It is worth including in a press release a short comment from, say, your organisation's chairperson or someone who is featured in the story. This means that a journalist using the press release can 'quote' directly from the individual concerned and give the appearance of an interview having taken place.

- **Provide an expert**. A number of charities and campaigning organisations (especially those devoted to medicine, health or the environment) have their own specialists who can be called on to comment on anything that relates to their subject. The press like this if the person sounds and/or looks good over the air and has enough genuineness to be regarded as accurate (even though not impartial).

ACTIVITY 4.4

Here's a press release from an organisation involved in winning resources and support. Spend about five minutes reading it and answering the question which follows:

Oakfield Community School
Acorn Lane
Treebourne

30 June

Press Release

For the attention of The Editor

The Oaktree School Parent Teacher Association have pleasure in announcing this year's Summer Family Fun Day which will take place on July 10 from 12 midday to 5pm.

The Day will be full of fantastic fun-filled events for all the family. After it is opened by retired local footballer, Alf Thyme, the day will include a series of games and attractions including traditional crafts and dancing displays, music and refreshments. There will be stalls selling a selection of bric-a-brac, nearly-new clothes, and cakes.

Proceeds will go towards our fundraising target this year – maintenance for the infant school roof.

The Summer Family Fun Day will be open to everybody in the area, and we sincerely hope that your newspaper will help to publicise this lovely occasion.

Yours

Sam Smith
Secretary of the OSPTA

As a journalist, how would you respond to this? Write a list of some ways in which it could be made more effective as a press release.

_____
_____
_____
_____
_____
_____
_____
_____
_____
_____
_____
_____
_____
_____
_____
_____
_____
_____
_____
_____
_____
_____
_____
_____
_____
_____
_____
_____

One reaction to the press release as a journalist might be that of frustration. There appears to be a story there, it's local and it has potential. But – apart from the local nature of the event, and the ex-footballer opening it, there is little here to act as a hook. The writing style is straightforward enough, but there is nothing to fasten on as a quotation. There could be lots more facts, and fewer opinions. A journalist might well resent being told in a press release that an event is 'fantastic' or 'lovely'.

Here is the same news story but in a more user-friendly press release:

Oakfield Community School
Acorn Lane
Treebourne

Press Release: 30 June for immediate use

Head teacher in the stocks

Ever wanted to throw wet sponges at your head teacher?

That's just one of the exciting things you can do at the Summer Family Fun Day at Oakfield Community School on July 10 from midday to 5pm. As part of the fun, Mr Len Dahande the school's head teacher will be put in the stocks – wet sponges available at 50p a throw. Mr Dahande commented yesterday:

'This year's Summer Family Fun Day is bigger and better than ever before. It's a chance to let our hair down with our families and friends in the local community. If the weather is as hot as last year, I will enjoy the sponges as much as the throwers do!'

Kicking off proceedings at the 12 midday opening ceremony is Alf Thyme, Treebourne United Football Club's top goal-scorer in their 1984/5 cup-winning season. Alf, who captained the school soccer team in the 1960s, commented:

'I am very honoured to be asked to open the Fun Day, and hope to see as many of my old friends there as possible.'

Funds raised will go towards maintenance work on the infant school roof. As Mr Dahande commented: 'I'd rather get soaked myself than have the roof leaking on the infants!'

Note to editor:

There will be a press photo call with Alf Thyme, Mr Dahande and the school steel band at 11.30am before the official opening.

For further information contact Oakfield School Parent Teacher Association Secretary Sam Smith
(01234) 567890 (office hours 8.30am to 4.30pm Monday - Friday)
email: sams@oakfieldpta.org.uk
Internet: http://www.oakfieldpta.org.uk/press

Spend a few minutes listing the points which make this a more effective press release than the first one.

Some features you might note are as follows:

- *full details of where/who the release is from with email/ phone contacts and a website*
- *clear date and sub-heading to establish the story immediately (although the eventual headline writer will probably be a sub-editor rather than the journalist him or herself)*
- *punchy quotes with an upbeat tone*
- *follow-up details – as well as an invitation to a photo opportunity*
- *logical layout and succinct writing style.*

> *It is clearer and more user-friendly than the first version. It gets to the point immediately, is quotable and has some nice hooks (the fact that Alf is an old boy of the school is a good detail, missed by the first press release).*
>
> (Source: adapted from Jempson and Williams, n.d.)

Of course, newspapers and other media don't just carry news stories of the sort that are generated from press releases. Other pages, often further on into the publication or in special sections devoted to leisure or travel, carry what are known as feature articles. These tend to be longer than most news stories, and less dependent on something that is happening here and now. They still have to be relevant to readers' interests, however. By either drafting an article (being careful to observe the style of your target publication), or doing some research and talking to a journalist in detail about an idea, you can reach key audiences through a carefully placed feature article. One of the great advantages of this is that you can go into a lot more detail than is possible in a shorter article. A compelling and relevant image to accompany the words makes the communication even more effective. Box 4.2 gives an example of how this can work in practice.

BOX 4.2

TWO OUT OF THREE ISN'T BAD

Age Concern England, a charity working to advance the welfare of older people, earns income from a number of specially tailored financial services. These include an insurance scheme for the over-50s and a funeral plan service. When working for a local branch of the charity some years ago, I got to know one of the journalists on the Women's Page of the local weekly newspaper, which had a very high circulation and readership in the branch's area. I drafted a feature article for her giving details about the insurance scheme, but focusing on the difficulties faced by older women in getting the right kinds of financial and other services. She rewrote the beginning and ending and shortened it a little, and it then appeared in the paper with an excellent photograph of our local shop manager holding an insurance leaflet. This worked really well in increasing awareness of the scheme and leaflet uptake. A few months later we did a similar piece of collaborative journalism about the funeral plan – this time with the angle that women tend to live longer than men. The story ran, with similar effects on awareness and enquiries.

However, I did not get very far with my attempt to pitch a third story to her about an initiative by the charity to earn income from 'Grandparents' Day' cards. I saw this as a useful income stream and a way of raising the profile of the increasingly important role that grandparents play in modern families. My journalist colleague, however, dismissed it as yet another way (alongside Mother's Day and Father's Day) for unscrupulous greetings card manufacturers to fleece a gullible public of children and grandchildren!

Broadcast media

Much of what we have said about spotting a good news angle or writing a press release applies as closely to television and radio journalism as it does to newspapers. Television, of course, needs pictures, and without a really strong visual angle your story will not get considered by an editor. However, if you can think one up, or even supply pre-recorded audio-visual material, as in the case of Barnardos in Box 4.3, you can go some way to having your good cause portrayed in a way which suits your mission. Even then, because television thrives on drama and conflict, you may find that your message is oversimplified or curtailed. The potential exposure to large numbers of people, however, even on a local news programme, makes aiming at television coverage attractive to most voluntary organisations.

BOX 4.3

MEDIA SAVVY

Barnardos, like many charities, has a campaigning as well as a service-delivery role. It has been keen to challenge media portrayal of children being sexually abused as 'child prostitutes' (a designation which implies their deliberate choice to be sex workers). This has involved:

making the issue a priority in discussions with journalists, to bring them round to an appreciation of how important language is in this context

being prepared to repeat the message to prevent it getting diluted or lost

supplying video images so that television news reports matched the reality of the situation which Barnardos saw in its projects rather than the stereotypes which the media tended to use otherwise.

(Source: adapted from Kingham and Coe, 2005)

Radio and television news and current affairs can be an extremely rewarding medium. Because of the range of topics covered by such programmes, they are always on the look out for 'experts' to interview. Interviews can, however, be stressful occasions. Des Wilson (1984) recommends being particularly wary of television journalists in this respect: 'Before you do a television interview, reflect for a moment or two on the main message you wish to convey in the interview. No matter what question you are asked, find a way of conveying that message' (p. 91). Interviewers are not necessarily antagonistic – but it pays to prepare carefully in order to get your message across simply and effectively so that people hearing it for the first time will understand. Involve the interviewer or the researcher who contacts you in your preparation, by asking questions about their understanding of the subject. Brief them in advance with written information as appropriate.

In turn, find out beforehand about the circumstances of the interview (e.g. will it be live or recorded, will the programme feature other interviews on the subject, how long is the planned slot?). This will help put you at ease and lead to a better outcome. If you are phoned for an immediate quote, make sure you are confident of your facts before giving one. If not, politely tell the journalist that you will phone back in ten minutes once you have gathered your information. Be sure to do so, however. Journalists tend to work under intense time pressure and if they cannot find out what they want from one source, they will quickly find another.

Box 4.4 outlines some essential advice for confident media interviews that enable you to put your organisation's case as succinctly and positively as possible using the 3 Cs and A, B, C, D:

BOX 4.4

GIVING A MEDIA INTERVIEW

During the interview

Remember the 3Cs principle:

Confidence

Have confidence in your own knowledge. You know your subject better than the journalist.

Clarity

Use a clear, conversational style. Establish a maximum of three key messages and illustrate your points with anecdotal examples for colour and credibility. Avoid jargon.

Control

Take charge of the interview. Preparation is the key. There is no such thing as a wrong question, only wrong answers.

Use the ABCD technique:

A Acknowledge and address the question (1 second)
e.g. yes, no, I don't know, I'm not able to answer that ...

B Bridge (3 seconds)
e.g. but, however, what I can tell you is ..., let's be clear about this ...

C Control and clarity (30 seconds)
e.g. key messages from your interview brief

D Dangle
e.g. what's really interesting is ...

Give examples

A good example can be worth a thousand words. People love stories so identify a graphic example or anecdote to back up every assertion.

Use analogies

Analogies are another good way to 'ring a bell' in the minds of the audience. Relate abstract terms and dimensions to everyday things e.g. converting hectares into football pitches.

Give advice

People love to be 'in the know'. Therefore, where possible give the audience a few hot tips on how to get the best out of something or to avoid disaster.

Anticipate questions

Don't worry too much about being asked a surprise question. There is a finite number of questions that can be asked on your subject and you're in a better position to know them than the journalist.

Body language

Bum in the back of the chair, lean forward, use your hands to communicate.

Don't discuss

It will make you sound too equivocal.

Don't defend

At least, not in such a way to make you sound defensive.

Don't debate

This lowers yourself and your organisation. The only exception to this is a panel debate.

It's your show

Every interview presents a golden opportunity to communicate your position to a large number of people. In thoroughly preparing your brief you are preparing the messages you are going to get across to the audience

(Source: Media Trust, 2007a)

ACTIVITY 4.5

Interviews with politicians, sports people and business leaders are a staple ingredient of news programmes on the radio. Presenters are rated on their ability to fire uncomfortable questions at public figures. But most public figures are exceptionally good at the three Cs of Confidence, Clarity and Control.

Pay careful attention to such an interview the next time you find yourself listening to a news programme. If possible record it, or 'listen again' on a website such as http://www.bbc.co.uk/radio4/today/listenagain/. See if you can recognise the sequence of A, B, C, D in how the person interviewed handles the questions:

Acknowledge and address the question (1 second)

Bridge (3 seconds)

Control and clarify (up to 30 seconds)

Dangle ....

Keep the customer in mind

Successful media relations are rather like successful marketing. You need to satisfy the needs of your customer (the journalist) in a way which benefits both parties. A good way of doing this is to consider the needs of the journalist's customers first (the readers, listeners or viewers who pay for the media in question through cover price, subscription or licence fee). Reading your target newspapers regularly, listening to and watching relevant radio and television programmes, and browsing appropriate websites should give you a clear idea of the kind of material which journalists working in each medium feel satisfies their customers' needs.

This process is not unlike the market research we discussed in the previous session. The resulting information will allow you to segment the available media in a way which helps you to set priorities for coverage and provide the relevant media outlets with the most appropriate material. The most important media will be those which are most popular with your key stakeholders. How far your organisation wishes to spread its media relations net will depend on its objectives and resources. However, it is probably better to work effectively with a limited number of media contacts than to try to keep in touch with too many.

4.1.2 Personal communication

The main advantage of personal vehicles of communication is that the message can be fine-tuned to the interests of the particular person, group or organisation being addressed. As a result there is a greater chance that the message will receive your audience's attention and be understood. Many forms of personal communication also allow a degree of interaction by you and your audience, so the recipient has a chance to clarify the message with the sender; there is also the potential for developing an ongoing relationship.

There are a number of different vehicles for personal communication, which vary according to how much personal interaction they allow.

Face-to-face communication

Direct face-to-face communication among a small group of people is the most personal and allows the most interaction. The personal approach – be it on the doorstep, at a function or in a meeting – remains the most direct and effective way of trying to persuade someone to make a donation, volunteer or otherwise support your cause. You can ask questions and learn from the answers, use eye contact and body language, and use your personality to establish rapport.

Of course, the disadvantage is that face-to-face communication entails considerable cost and commitment, and is therefore unsuitable for reaching a mass audience unless you have an army of volunteers who can, for example, carry out door-to-door collections or membership drives. Mass personal solicitation of regular donations has a role in fundraising, as illustrated in Box 4.5. However, if you are looking for big gifts, negotiating an important deal or lobbying important people, face-to-face communication will be essential. It is also critically important to make sure you choose the *right person* to make the communication.

BOX 4.5

THE RISE OF THE CHUGGERS

Groups of smiling young people, wearing fluorescent tabards and clutching clipboards are becoming a regular sight on city streets and stations. Catch the eye of one and you will be warmly greeted, asked how you are, and whether you have a few minutes to spare about cancer relief (or whatever the client charity happens to be) and, in all likelihood, signed up to a direct debit to support the good cause. The chugger (short for 'charity mugger') is a relatively new import to the world of fundraising in the UK. Pioneered by Greenpeace in 1997, 'Face-to-face' or 'Direct-dialogue' fundraising has since become the fastest growing fundraising technique in Britain.

The teams of fundraisers are recruited by companies signed up with the Public Fundraising Regulatory Authority (PFRA) and trained both how to ask for regular support and about the good causes on whose behalf they are working. They are paid and are obliged to point out that they are not volunteers when soliciting donations. Because the companies for whom they are working have contracts to raise specific amounts of money for the charities which use them, the chuggers have to achieve a minimum recruitment of regular donors each day. It works out in real terms at two 'sign-ups' per day – but, as more and more of those who are willing to offer regular support do so, the pool of potential ⮕

support may be dwindling. Staff turnover is, predictably, high. Nevertheless, in 2002, 350,000 members of the public set up direct debits with chuggers.

Liz Monks, deputy director of fundraising at Shelter, points to the communication benefits of the technique as well as its effectiveness in raising money: 'Shelter is very misunderstood. We are not only about helping people on the street but also helping people to stay in housing. With face-to-face, people are trained before they go out so they can tell people about us.'

But many commuters and shoppers regard the chugger as the sort of hazard you have to cross the street to avoid. Antony Robbins, head of communications at the Charity Commission, reflects 'People don't like being buttonholed on the street. It is seen as aggressive.' On the other hand, he admits, 'Many people find it a pain but if you don't want to give on the street then don't.' In fact, if there is any aggression involved it tends to be directed at the chugger rather than part of the sales pitch. Robbins admits 'People verbally or occasionally physically attack fundraisers. It is very disappointing.'

(Source: Asthana, 2003; Burrows, 2002)

Personal correspondence, email and calls

You can also carry out a personal dialogue with someone at a distance using the telephone or various methods of correspondence (e.g. emails, letters, memos, faxes). Telephone and electronic media have the advantage of immediacy – you can respond straight away to what someone is saying. On the other hand, it is difficult to give a detailed message over the phone. Written correspondence such as email is much better for this purpose, and provides a tangible record of what has been communicated.

Personal correspondence and calls are often used to complement face-to-face communication, perhaps to prepare for a meeting or to put on record what has happened. The advantage over more mass forms of communication such as telemarketing or direct mail is that your message can be targeted to meet a particular individual's needs and concerns.

The AIDA model is helpful in structuring calls and correspondence. Another useful guide to saving your own and other people's time when writing letters and short reports is provided by Green (1999) who, appropriately enough for communication aimed at minimising paper, suggests the SCRAP approach. This provides a framework to help you be sure of covering what you need in the minimum number of words, and getting the desired response – and can be adapted to structuring phone calls and emails as well as letters and memos. The sequence is: Situation, Complication/Concern, Resolution/Recommendation, Action and Politeness.

For example, you could be writing to a supplier about an order that has gone wrong or has been delayed. You would begin by stating the situation. Here it would be a reminder of the original order. The complication or concern would be about what has happened (or not happened) since. The recommendation might be, in this case, to extract a promise of delivery by a particular date or threaten the cancellation of the order (action on your part unless there is action on theirs). Politeness would be particularly useful in this situation in order to maintain a tone of friendly assertiveness rather than antagonistic aggression.

Conferences, meetings and events

Speaking or having a stand at conferences, meetings and events are other ways of delivering your message. They are ways of reaching a particular group of people with some scope for personal interaction and follow-up. These events may range in scale and scope from addressing a small local meeting to large international conferences or conventions, depending on your area of work and who you need to influence. For those involved in public relations or campaigning they can be a particularly useful way of quickly reaching key opinion formers, such as journalists, politicians or experts in particular fields.

Costs will vary according to the nature of the event, but can be steep. If your organisation is sending people to a large conference there will be the costs of preparing any materials, costs of travel, costs of the conference, the costs of people involved, and so on. So it is important to think carefully about how you are going to use the opportunity, and whether or not it is a good investment, and to be selective about which opportunities are taken up.

It is worth developing a resource such as a short video or PowerPoint presentation for use when addressing groups. If you can train a number of volunteers to give a talk about your organisation you will have a very valuable channel for reaching community groups and local associations. Just as the journalists referred to in the last section need a constant supply of news material, so local groups and associations need visiting speakers. Furthermore, if you can engage them successfully with your organisation or good cause, they can provide energetic fundraising support and community involvement. Again, the AIDA model is a useful outline when planning and delivering presentations to groups.

4.1.3 Personalised communication

There is a further category of communication which, while it has the potential to reach a large number of people (in the same way as impersonal media do) nevertheless addresses them as individuals through personalisation, as in Box 4.6. This process involves the tailoring of communication specifically to large numbers of recipients – often with their active involvement in either requesting or limiting the extent and form of the communication.

BOX 4.6

PERSONALISED SERVICE FROM GREENPEACE

Greenpeace believe that the internet is similar in many ways to other fundraising channels in that there are costs, response percentages, average gifts, and other measurable features. So – as with any other promotional activity – for the internet Greenpeace sets measurable benchmarks and goals, defines what is to be measured, sets controlled tests, and measures success in the usual way. The organization's visitor relationship management project set out to establish whether a more personalized, individual electronic relationship would produce supporters who are more satisfied, more loyal, and more profitable to Greenpeace than those developed via other methods – and at a lower cost to service and support.

Greenpeace reasoned that, whereas there is plenty of evidence that personalization enhances donor relationships, the cost of detailed personalization often outweighs its benefits offline. But that cost would be substantially lower and therefore well worthwhile online. Indeed it might be both possible and beneficial to personalize not just appeals but e-newsletters and Web pages too. Participants would be asked at every opportunity for appropriate information that could be used later to improve the depth of personalization and increase the feeling of an individual experience.

(Source: Burnett, 2002, p. 301)

Direct mail

Direct mail enables organisations to identify and target specific groups by sending personally addressed communications to them. The recipient has an opportunity to tailor what is received, not only by choosing which parts to read and which to reject, but by actively agreeing such communication. This happens when someone is offered inclusion on a mailing list. Lists, or databases as they are also known, are central to the information management which drives direct mail. The popularity of the technique has grown in step with the increasing sophistication (and falling costs) of computerised databases. Some organisations capture detailed histories of every supporter's donation patterns. The more sophisticated users of direct mail use this information as a resource to better appreciate what kinds of mailing work best with which sorts of group. It is particularly useful in developing relationships with existing donors and supporters, rather than as a recruitment tool (Brackin, 2007).

There are many excellent books and training opportunities on direct mail and other forms of direct marketing using different media, as well as a burgeoning number of expert specialist agencies. We do not have the space or scope to do more than touch on this highly technical subject here. However, because of the crucial role played by writing in direct mail, much of what we have said in the last session about persuasive communication, style and image, and message delivery holds true for this technique.

Email and viral marketing

Email and other electronic media can establish a powerful personal connection with donors and supporters – offering them the opportunity to opt into regular newsletters, action alerts and updates on particular campaigns or activities. This requires the organization to be committed to collecting email addresses from donors and supporters at every possible opportunity. However, such information dates rapidly because of the frequency with which many people change their email address – so an active relationship needs to be sought. Stanford University found that recipients of its alumni e-newsletter (@Stanford) were significantly more likely to make donations than people with whom it had offline communication (Sargeant and Jay, 2004, p. 287).

Viral marketing is a way of piggybacking on other people's email communication, like a virus in a system. It involves creating some kind of gimmick or email attachment (such as a short video clip) which people enjoy so much that they want to pass it on to friends and colleagues. The popularity of email means that a message can spread rapidly among a large number of users. For a fundraising or campaigning organisation the trick is to devise something which is not only engaging and shareable, but has direct relevance to your brand. Box 4.7 shows how a charity used viral marketing to heighten awareness of its cause, but such a technique could also include an opportunity to donate.

BOX 4.7

THE SECRET SEX GLAND

The Prostate Cancer Charity launched an online game 'Journey to Planet Prostate' as part of its ongoing campaign to raise awareness about the prostate gland. Given that one in 13 men face diagnosis with prostate cancer, the idea was to arm players with facts about this part of the body to make them more receptive of future health messages. The game involves visiting a website (Planetprostate.com) to help Sammy the Sperm through various challenges in his voyage from the twin planets of Testes. BBC Online picked up on the game which then reached hundreds of thousands of people worldwide.

(Source: adapted from Prostate Cancer Charity, 2003)

Telemarketing

Telemarketing (or telephone marketing) offers many of the advantages of personal communication, but at considerably less cost. The personal touch means that response rates are usually higher than with techniques such as direct mail. Outbound telephone marketing (where the organisation rings the potential donor) can be used for member and volunteer recruitment (for example ringing known supporters to ask for their help in house-to-house collections) to solicit donations, and to prepare supporters for the launch of a direct mail campaign. The technique has been successfully used by a number of universities to contact alumni in the context of appeals. Often the calls are made by current students in order to make the request more personal and authentic.

Telephones may also be used to receive donations (an example of what is known as inbound calling). For example, local-rate numbers may be established to receive pledges or credit card donations during major appeals. As with any intrusive medium, however, the telephone needs to be used with care. Properly trained operators, and careful targeting and timing of calls, pay dividends both in goodwill and income.

Mobile telephony has added a new dimension to personal communication since the late 1990s, as not only speech but text, sound and images are transferred between users on the move. SMS (Short Messaging Service) text messaging offers non-profit organisations a number of advantages over more traditional media. It has high urgency (texts are usually read immediately), response-capability (direct from the receiver's phone) and low cost (texting is cheaper than direct mail or telemarketing). Furthermore, it is popular with the elusive younger donor or patron (Phillips, 2002.) Fundraising applications include the ability to donate by texting to a particular number, whereupon a sum is transferred to the relevant good cause and shown on the phone-owner's next bill.

Privacy

All of the communication techniques we have reviewed in this session involve the collection and use of information to a greater or lesser extent. But many individuals value their privacy. Any sense that it is being infringed risks violating the trust that is essential to the donor or supporter relationship. Telemarketing, direct mail and internet marketing raise concerns because of the power of computers to store and manipulate vast amounts of personal data, but collecting data of any sort involves ethical issues of privacy. UK data protection legislation protects the rights of individuals to see data stored on them, correct any mistakes in it and prevent it being used for marketing purposes should they so desire. The words of the UK legislation state that information needs to be 'fairly processed' – for example it cannot be collected covertly on individuals. All data controllers (i.e. individuals in organisations who collect, store and manipulate personal data) need to be registered with the Information Commissioner. The detail of the UK Data Protection Act is beyond the scope of this course, but comprehensive information is available from http://www.ico.gov.uk/. The basic principles laid down in the Act are reproduced in Box 4.8. Legislation based on similar principles either exists or is in the process of being evolved in other countries as well, so this is a useful site for international fundraisers keen to establish good practice in this area.

BOX 4.8

THE PRINCIPLES OF DATA PROTECTION

Anyone processing personal data must comply with the eight enforceable principles of good practice. These state that data must be:

- fairly and lawfully processed
- processed for limited purposes
- adequate, relevant and not excessive
- accurate
- not kept longer than necessary
- processed in accordance with the data subject's rights
- secure
- not transferred to other countries without adequate protection.

(Source: http://www.ico.gov.uk/)

4.1.4 Deciding your communication mix

As you have seen so far, there is a variety of different vehicles that can be used to communicate with your audiences. Very often it is not sensible to rely solely on one vehicle which might be missed or ignored – you will want to integrate a mix of different vehicles which complement each other and reinforce your message to your target audiences. So it is important to think through what this mix should be and how you should allocate resources to the elements within it.

One of the first considerations will be the characteristics of the audience that you want to reach. The *size* of your audience, where it is *located*, its *preferences*, will all have to be taken into account. For example, if your audience is local to one area or region it will not be sensible to advertise in the national press: an approach that uses local media will usually be more appropriate. You will need to think through what media members of your audience are most likely to read, watch or listen to. If you don't know, you may need to carry out some market research to find out.

The *characteristics of the message* you want to communicate will have an influence too. If your message is long and complex it will not be suitable for many forms of advertising, for example posters, television or radio.

The decision will need to take account of the *resources* available, especially cost. Forms of communication that use the mass media are cheaper in terms of cost per thousand people reached than are more personalised forms of communication. However, this is not the whole story. High initial costs for TV and press advertising may put these vehicles beyond the reach of many organisations. More importantly, while mass media advertising may be an efficient means of reaching people it is not necessarily the most effective in achieving the desired response.

It is important, then, to look at effectiveness as well as cost. As a general rule of thumb, if you are trying to persuade someone to give, the more personalised the vehicle of communication is, the more effective it is likely to be. However, personalised methods are also the most expensive

An important factor to consider when deciding the communication mix is how the various elements will integrate so that they complement and reinforce each other. This idea of getting the right mix can be applied at different levels – when planning a particular event, appeal or campaign, or when putting together longer-term plans for your unit or organisation. For example, if you are putting on a news conference you may want to provide journalists with an information pack containing additional information and photographs they can use in putting together a story. A major appeal, such as the NSPCC's Full Stop campaign, will involve a complex mix of media and techniques aimed at an interlaced network of donors and supporters, from modest sums donated by pensioners to the enormous gifts of 'high net worth' individuals usually associated with appeals in the arts and education rather than social welfare (Mullin, 2002, P. 95).

ACTIVITY 4.6

Consider an event, appeal or campaign that your organisation, or one that you are familiar with, has recently been involved with.

(a) Who were the main target audiences?

_____

_____

_____

(b) What was the communication mix used to reach these audiences?

_____

_____

_____

_____

(c) Do you think the mix could have been improved in any way? Give reasons for your answer.

4.2 FUNDRAISING AND CAMPAIGNING

Baguley (2007) points out 'the word "campaign" is used indiscriminately in fundraising to describe the application of almost any fundraising technique' (p. 74). He pins down the meaning of the word, however, to cover activity which goes outside the existing donor base of the charity to mobilise public support on a wider scale using the media. There is also a sense in which 'campaign' used in this way refers to a coordinated programme of activity over time with a particular objective. Baguley distinguishes between 'opportunistic' and 'planned' fundraising campaigns. Opportunistic campaigns are responses to events (a natural disaster, for example) which build on existing media coverage to channel aid to emergency relief and longer-term reconstruction. Planned campaigns, by contrast, have to generate media coverage in order to bring a problem to light and thus pave the way for its solution through winning the appropriate resources and support. A good example in the UK is the work of the NSPCC. Its 'Full Stop' campaign has run since 1999 to highlight the realities of contemporary cruelty to children and to act as an overarching framework for the organisation's fundraising activity.

4.2.1 Winning political support

Both planned and opportunistic campaigns aim at winning more than just financial or material support. They are aimed at hearts and minds, at what we might call winning 'political support'. They use communication to further the mission of the charity in a way which does not necessarily involve service delivery direct to beneficiaries. This can be controversial. For example, the NSPCC encountered criticism from some quarters for spending money on advertising to bring child abuse to public attention rather than using it to fund more services for abused children, even though the organisation's remit has always included carrying out 'publicity and educational work of all descriptions' (*Guardian*, 2000).

This kind of 'campaigning' is defined by Kingham and Coe (2005) as 'the mobilisation of forces by organisations to influence others in order to effect an identified and desired social, economic, environmental or political change' (p. 5). Depending on the size and nature of your organisation your fundraising communication may overlap with this kind of campaigning work, or it may be completely separate and, in some ways, even difficult to reconcile with it.

UK charity law forbids charities from being constituted to pursue political purposes, and the expectation that charities should be non-partisan in political matters is widely shared throughout the world. On the other hand, campaigning (for example to raise awareness of child abuse) and/or political activity (aimed at changing the law or public policy on a particular issue such as road safety legislation) are perfectly legitimate activities for charities, provided:

- 'that the activities are relevant to the purposes of the charity as set out in the governing documents
- that they are an effective means of furthering the purposes of the charity
- that the resources applied are proportional with achieving the aims of the campaign' (Lamb, 2005, p. 209)

Whatever the legal situation, if donors are motivated to give by the prospect of funding specific services to alleviate immediate problems, they may object to seeing their money applied to longer-term and indirect strategies such as lobbying and policy work – no matter how central to the organisation's mission.

This is why organisations need to integrate fundraising communications with communications aimed at furthering educational or policy objectives, rather than treating the two separately. This is a challenging prospect. For example, fundraising mailings or events have to be planned a long time in advance, whereas 'political' campaigning is often reactive to the turn of recent news and emerging opportunities. There is also a management cost involved in trying to integrate communications across an organisation – complicating and lengthening approval processes. But involving supporters, members and volunteers in campaigning can be a way of reinforcing their commitment as donors.

Many organisations which begin by offering direct services to alleviate the effects of social problems evolve towards campaigning in order to highlight and address the causes of the problems (Kingham and Coe, 2005, p. 130). Examples in the UK include charities with their roots in Victorian philanthropy, such as the Children's Society and the YWCA, as well as development charities, such as Oxfam. Other charities are firmly at the 'philanthropic' end, such as hospices and museums. Others, again, are very much at the 'political' end, such as the UK development charity War on Want. And, of course, there are pressure groups and political organisations whose orientation to campaigning is such that they do not qualify for charitable status under current legislation. Figure 4.1 presents service provision (the focus of most charities' fundraising) and campaigning (in the 'political' sense just referred to) as two ends of a continuum.

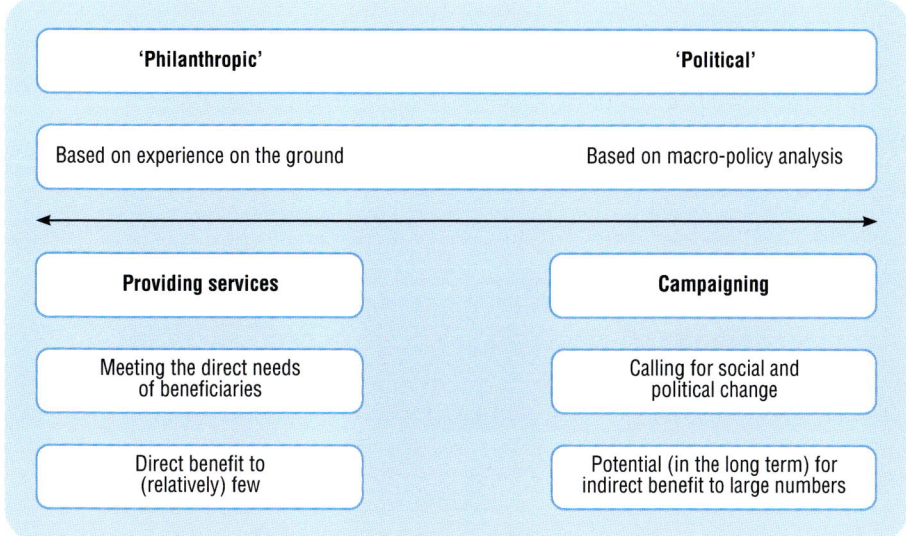

Figure 4.1 Twin-track approach to achieving social change (Source: Kingham and Coe, 2005, p. 109)

Campaigns, whether for fundraising or more generally, can have private and public aspects. Much of the impact that charities and pressure groups have on government policy is a result of lobbying key decision makers and contributing through research, information and consultation. This work happens away from the public gaze, just as the early stages of a capital appeal will be spent quietly securing major gifts and grants to give the project solidity before the launch of the public phase. But mobilising public support is an essential element of all opportunistic campaigns and of most other campaigns at some stage. Baguley (2007) highlights a model called the 'Campaign Diamond' setting out four key factors which affect how successful such mobilisation is likely to be from one situation to another:

For a diagram of the Campaign Diamond, see Thoughtful Fundraising, the Course Reader, p. 76.

1 The problem or needs: how clearly articulated and urgent the objective of the campaign is.

2 The social authorisation for the campaign – in other words, the level of consensus on the importance of the objective of the campaign. This comes from, for example, the fact that it has attracted media coverage or comment from opinion leaders, such as politicians or celebrities.

3 Operational capacity: a factor internal to the organisation reflecting its ability to convert the 'hearts and minds' support generated by the campaign into something more tangible, such as donations, membership or action.

4 The opportunity for social value: the extent to which the organisation can show it can make a difference to the problem about which it is campaigning. Like any objective, the better defined the problem or needs behind the campaign the more likely it is that there will be a successful outcome. A track record of success adds to the campaigning organisation's credibility in this regard.

The 'Campaign Diamond' can help organisations assess the timing, focus, and even feasibility, of running a campaign. Another useful concept in understanding why and how campaigns work is to analyse the sources of political influence available to a voluntary or community organisation in a particular campaigning context. There are four main types, according to Keck and Sikkink (1998):

- Information politics: voluntary organisations have access to information which policy-makers value and would find hard to access unaided. This is a powerful bargaining tool.

- Symbolic politics: powerful images attract support and engage emotions, and can act as a kind of short-hand for more complex issues. The use of wristbands or ribbons by supporters to show solidarity is a good example of symbolism at work.

- Leverage politics: while many organisations, particularly smaller ones, lack direct access to decision makers, they will have networks and intermediaries which can be leveraged to exert influence.

- Accountability politics: organisations can 'shame' authorities into honouring commitments through public encouragement. Very occasionally this can apply to individuals – as, for example, when the UK's Royal Opera House threatened a major benefactor with the withdrawal of his name from a public space which had been named after him unless he honoured his pledged donations (*Guardian*, 2005). A fruitless threat, however, as the unfortunate individual had gone broke, leading to the cancellation of the deal.

ACTIVITY 4.7

(a) Thinking about your own organisation, or one with which you are familiar, where would you place it on the continuum between 'providing services' and 'campaigning' in Figure 4.1?

(b) How, if at all, has this changed over time?

(c) How has the organisation's fundraising approach been affected?

An example from the UK where a charity has expanded its campaigning work over the course of time is the Children's Society (originally founded in 1881), which set up a dedicated campaigning arm in 2004 following an internal review. The organisation's website describes its history in four broad phases of understanding and responding to changing needs: 'Children's Homes' up to the 1970s, 'Caring for Families' up to the 1990s, 'Achieving Social Justice' up to 2002, and from 2003, 'Concentrating on those groups who need us most' (Source: http://www.childrenssociety.org.uk). A potential risk of doing more campaigning is that the Society may come into conflict with key institution, such as local authorities, which are potential or actual funders and partners in its work.

4.2.2 Evaluating communication

How can you tell if your communication is working? Ultimately, by determining whether it is having the intended effect. Reilly (2007) emphasises the importance of starting with the end in mind:

> Always start by making yourself complete in writing the sentence, 'This piece of communication (e.g. feature article, exhibition, poster) will have achieved its objective if....' Really do write it out in black and white. It is often more difficult than you think. Try to achieve an action or measurable result as a result of your communication.

Sometimes the action or measurable result is clear to see. A mailing that achieves, or exceeds, its targeted level of donations is working. But sometimes the outcome is less easy, or practical, to measure. Issuing a press release about an event like a fundraising concert will, we hope, generate a certain amount of media coverage of the right sort, be seen by a certain number of people in our target group and result in the outcome of attendance. But how much weight can we give the press release in attracting audiences compared to, say, paid-for advertising or direct mail? One way of determining this might be to ask people who come to the concert about how they found out about it. But doing that regularly would consume a disproportionate amount of effort and time. Another way might be to focus not on the final outcome achieved by the press release (i.e. attendance attributable to it) but on what it achieves along the way in amount or nature of coverage. This is not the final outcome (as we mentioned earlier in this section, communication is not an end in itself) but an output which can be used as a proxy measure.

There are two ways of measuring such an output: quantitative and qualitative. Quantitative evaluation means counting 'how much' – for example how many stories and mentions, in how many publications. Given that advertising space has to be paid for, one way of estimating the monetary value of 'free' publicity in the media is to try and work out how much the equivalent advertising space (or broadcast time) would have cost. This is a very crude rule of thumb, as advertising and public relations are different ways of communicating. But it is useful if only as a morale booster.

Qualitative evaluation asks 'what kind' of coverage you have achieved. For example, what kind of publications or broadcasts have you managed to appear in, and how does that reflect coverage of your target audience? And how prominent has each appearance of the item been (was it a leading story, a feature, a brief mention, or a 'and finally...' piece. Crucially, what kind of message actually got across? Was it positive? Did it convey the key phrases you are trying to drive home? Reilly (2007) recommends developing a scoring system to assess quality of coverage based on the number of key messages communicated against a monthly target.

ACTIVITY 4.8

List below an external activity or event that your organisation, or one that you are familiar with, either already runs or might run in the future (e.g. a fundraising event, a visit by a funder to a project, a public meeting, etc.). Then describe what communications work you might expect to accompany it. Finally, suggest ways in which the communications in each case could be evaluated.

Event/Activity	Communications	Evaluation

4.3 SUMMARY

Here is a summary of the main learning points from this session:

- Impersonal communication (advertising, publications, public relations using the media) reaches large numbers with little or no individual variation.

- Personal communication (face-to-face, telephone, correspondence) is powerful but expensive.

- Personalised communication (direct mail, electronic media and telemarketing) harnesses information technology to reach large numbers with individual variation.

- Advertising uses paid-for media to inform and/or persuade potential and existing customers.

- Publications allow detailed information but make significant demands on resources.

- Public relations using the media allow you to 'piggyback' your message in print and broadcast media by aligning your needs to those of journalists.

- Newsworthiness depends on the freshness of a story and its 'angle' or perspective. Pictures, controversy, personalities and authoritative opinion promote newsworthiness.

- Feature articles depend less on immediacy than news stories, but are relevant to readers' interests.

- Media interviews need preparation and performance of the three Cs: Confidence, Clarity and Control. A useful structure for handling questions is A, B, C, D: Acknowledge and address the question, Bridge, Control and clarify, Dangle.

- A useful structure for memos, email and letters is SCRAP: state the Situation, outline the Complication or concern, make a Resolution or recommendation, indicate the Action required of the recipient, and maintain a Polite tone.

- Data protection law requires data to be:

  - fairly and lawfully processed

  - processed for limited purposes

  - adequate, relevant and not excessive

  - accurate

  - not kept longer than necessary

  - processed in accordance with the data subject's rights

  - secure

  - not transferred to other countries without adequate protection.

- Appropriate media choice depends on: audience and message characteristics, resources available and capacity for integration.

- Campaigns, either opportunistic (reacting to external events in the media) or planned (generating their own media coverage) aim to mobilise political and/or financial support beyond an organisation's existing base.

- Campaigning by charities must support their charitable objectives.

- The Campaign Diamond model helps organisations assess the feasibility of campaigning by interrogating the nature of the problem addressed and its social authorisation, compared with the organisation's internal capacity and ability to add social value.

- Campaigning organisations can draw on information, symbolic, leverage and accountability politics.

- Direct and proxy measures of effects are both useful in evaluating communication.

REFERENCES

Asthana, A. (2003) 'Your money – or their life', *The Observer*, 9 March.

Baguley, J. (2007) 'Fundraising Campaigns', in Mordaunt, J. and Paton, R. (eds) *Thoughtful Fundraising: Concepts, Issues and Perspectives*, London, Routledge with the OU Business School, pp. 74-81.

Bailey, G. (2000) 'LFF Focus GroupsFinal Report Spring 1999', The Listener-Focused Fundraising Project [online], http://www. aranet.com/library/pdf/doc-0101.pdf (Accessed 21 February 2007).

Brackin, J. (2007) 'Delivering the donors', *Professional Fundraising Magazine*, Supplement – Spotlight on Direct Mail Part 1, January, pp. 2–5.

Burnett, K. (2002) *Relationship Fundraising* (2nd edn) San Francisco, Jossey-Bass.

Burrows, G. (2002) 'Charities go corporate', *New Statesman*, 16 December.

Chartered Institute of Public Relations (2006) 'What is PR?' [online], http://www.ipr.org.uk/direct/careers.asp?v1=whatis (Accessed 20 February 2007).

Community Links (2007) 'Youth empowerment', 13 February [online], http://www.community-links.org/ourwork/ youthempower_page23.aspx (Accessed 20 February 2007).

Dibb, C.S., Simkin, L., Pride, W. and Ferrell, O.C. (2005) *Marketing: Concepts and Strategies* (5th edn), Boston, Houghton Mifflin.

Dyer, S., Buell, T., Harrison, M. and Weber, S. (2002) 'Managing Public Relations in Nonprofit Organisations', *Public Relations Quarterly*, Winter, vol. 47, issue 4, pp. 13–18.

Elischer, T. (1998) 'Get on yer cycle' [online], http://www.thinkcs. org/downloads/fundcyc.pdf (Accessed 21 February 2007).

Freeman, R.F. (1984) *Strategic Management*, Pitman.

Green, P. (1999) *Managing Time: Loving Every Minute*, Skills in Action Series, Cookham, Chartered Institute of Marketing.

Grieve, J. (2005) 'Marathon runners raise record sums online', Press Release, 15 April [online], http://www.justgiving.com/statements/ press/press_releases.asp# (Accessed 10 June 2005).

Guardian(2000) 'Charities need to account for our money', 9 December [online], http://society.guardian.co.uk/voluntary/story/ 0,,409844,00.html (Accessed 20 February 2007).

Hill, L., O'Sullivan, C. and O'Sullivan,T. (2003) *Creative Arts Marketing* (2nd edn), Oxford, Butterworth Heinemann.

Institute of Fundraising (2006) *The Good Fundraising Guide*, London, Institute of Fundraising; also available online at http://www.institute-of-fundraising.org.uk/documents/ good_fundraising_guide.pdf (Accessed 21 February 2007).

Jempson, M. and Williams, G. (n.d.) *Reaching the Media: a media guide for Yorkshire and Humberside*, Campaign for Press and Broadcasting Freedom.

Keck, M. and Sikkink, K. (1998) *Activists Beyond Borders: Advocacy Networks in International Politics*, Ithaca, NY, Cornell University Press.

Kingham, T. and Coe, J. (2005) *The Good Campaigns Guide*, London, National Council for Voluntary Organisations Publications.

Kotler, P. and Armstrong, G. (2008) *Principles of Marketing* (12th edn), Englewood Cliffs, NJ, Prentice Hall.

Kramer, P.L. (1998 '"New Employee Orientation Powerpoint", College of Agricultural, Human, and Natural Resource Sciences (CAHNRS) Alumni Office, Washington State University Fundraising and Capital campaigns – Powerpoint 11-10-05' [online], http:// www.cahealumni.wsu.edu/alumnidev/index.htm (Accessed 21 February 2007).

Lamb, B. (2005) 'Appendix – campaigning and political activities by charities' in Kingham and Coe (2005), pp. 209–13.

McDonald, M. and Dunbar, I. (2004) *Market Segmentation: how to do it, how to profit from it*, Oxford, Elsevier Butterworth Heinemann.

Media Trust (2007a) 'Giving a Media Interview' [online], http:// www.mediatrust.org/training-events/training-resources/online-guides-1/guide_giving-a-media-interview/(Accessed 20 February 2007).

Media Trust (2007b) 'Maintaining your site' [online], http://www. mediatrust.org/training-events/training-resources/online-guides-1/ guide_maintaining-your-site/(Accessed 20 February 2007).

Mullin, R. (2002) *Fundraising Strategy* (2nd edn), CAF/Directory of Social Change/Institute of Fundraising.

Oxfam (2004a) Stakeholder Survey 2003/4 [online], http:// www.oxfam.org.uk/about_us/downloads/survey2003-4.pdf (Accessed 20 February 2007).

Oxfam (2004b) CMT Response to Stakeholder Survey 2003/4 [online], http://www.oxfam.org.uk/about_us/downloads/SHS03.pdf (accessed 20 February 2007).

Pascal, B. (1997 [1657]) *The Provincial Letters*, Wipf and Stock Publishers.

Phillips, A. (2002) 'SMS: the benefits', *Journal of Arts Marketing*, issue 6, July, p. 17.

Prostate Cancer Charity (2003) Annual Review 2003: Sharpening our focus ... [online], http://www.prostate-cancer.org.uk/aboutUs/images/ pccAnnualReview2003.pdf (Accessed 10 June 2005).

Reed, P.B. and Selbee, L. K. (2001) 'The civic core in Canada: disproportionality in charitable giving, volunteering, and civic participation', *Nonprofit and Voluntary Sector Quarterly*, vol. 30, no. 4, December, pp. 761–80.

Reilly, J. (2007) 'Top PR Tips' [online], http://www.mediatrust.org/training-events/training-resources/online-guides-1/guide_top-pr-tips/ (Accessed 20 February 2007).

Rosso, H. (2003) *Achieving Excellence in Fundraising*, (2nd edn), San Francisco, Jossey-Bass.

Royal Opera House (2005) 'Vilar Floral Hall reverts to being called Floral Hall', Press Release [online], http://info.royaloperahouse.org/News/Index.cfm?ccs=892&highlight=vilar (Accessed 20 February 2007).

Sargeant, A. (1999) 'Charitable giving: towards a model of donor behaviour', *Journal of Marketing Management*, vol. 15, pp. 215–38.

Sargeant, A. and Jay, E. (2003) 'The Fundraising Performance of Charity Websites: A US/UK Comparison', *Interactive Marketing*, vol. 4, no. 4, pp. 330–42.

Sargeant, A. and Jay, E. (2004) *Fundraising Management*, London, Routledge.

Schramm, W. (1954) cited in Watson, J. (1998) *Media Communication*, London, Macmillan, p. 37.

Seymour, H.J. (1966) *Designs for Fund-raising: principles, patterns, techniques*, New York, McGraw Hill.

Visible Voices (2007) [online] http://www.communitylinks.co.uk/voices.html (Accessed 20 February 2007).

Wilson, D. (1984) *Pressure: The A–Z of campaigning in Britain*, London, Heinemann.

Wolverton, B. (2002) 'Reading donors', *The Chronicle of Philanthropy*, 3 October, p. 29.

World YWCA Common Concern (2000) *YMCA Fundraising – the Case for Support*, September [online], http://worldywca1.org/common_concern/sept2000/Case.html (Accessed 21 February 2007).

ACKNOWLEDGEMENTS

Grateful acknowledgement is made to the following sources for permission to include material within this book:

Cover Image: © Digital Vision / Getty Images

Text

Box 1.2: YWCA Fundraising, 'The Case for Support' from *Common Concern* September 2000, reproduced with permission from YWCA England and Wales; *Box 3.1:* Adapted from Kingham, T. and Coe, J. (2005) *The Good Campaigns Guide: Campaigning for Impact*, © NCVO; *Box 4.1:* Media Trust, 'Maintaining your site", http://www.mediatrust.org/training-events-resources/online-guides-1/guide_maintaining-your-site, © Media Trust; *Box 4.4:* Media Trust, 'Giving a media interview', http://www.mediatrust.org/training-events-resources/online-guides-1/guide_giving-a-media-interview, © Media Trust

Figures

Figure 2.1: Copyright © Community Links/www.community-links.org; *Figure 3.1:* Courtesy of the Royal National Lifeboat Institution; *Figure 4.1:* Kingham, T. and Coe, J. (2005) The Good Campaigns Guide: Campaigning for Impact, © NCVO;